THE BEST THINGS MOTHERS DO

Susan Isaacs Kohl

Dedication

To Carol, who showed us that it's the compassionate action of "all of us taking care of all of us" that will lead us into a new, more beautiful world; and beloved Murshid Walker, who encouraged me to discover that writing can be prayer;

About the Author

For thirty years, Susan Isaacs Kohl has been one of the directors of The White Pony/Meher Schools, a place where "love nurtures learning" and adults and children collaborate to create caring community and, by extension, a more caring world. Meher means compassion. She writes a weekly column for her school community and beyond called *Parenting from the Heart*. Susan is the author of six parenting books: *The Inner Parent*, with Marti Keller; *Who's in Control? How to Organize Your Child's Room; I Think I Can, I Know I Can*, with Dr. Wendy Ritchey; *The Best Things Parents Do;* and *The Best Things Mothers Do: How Big Picture Thinking Awakens Us to What Matters and Relieves Anxiety and Stress.*

She has written numerous articles for *Parents Magazine, Family Circle, Diablo Magazine,* and the *San Francisco Chronicle,* has been a guest on the *Today Show* made numerous appearances on local TV and radio. She received a master's degree in education, working with the renowned early childhood educator and author, Dr. Mary Lane. For years, Susan taught college early childhood education classes and has been a consultant for Head Start and the National Association of Education for Young Children. Susan has worked with parents to see the big picture of their children's development since she was twenty-one. She is a self-confessed parent watcher and appreciator and enjoys nothing more than hearing parents' amazing stories of growth.

Susan has three children who are wonderful parents and five grandchildren who keep her excited about life daily through their surprising adventures.

Forward

Wendy Ritchey, PhD

Co-author, *I think I Can, I know I Can*

It was over thirty years ago that I first met Susan Isaacs Kohl. I was newly licensed in California and was anxious to begin my private practice as a child psychologist. I was also the mother of a two-year-old boy, and I had definite ideas about the kind of child care I wanted for him when I was working: the school needed to be grounded on sound principles of child development, and the caregivers had to love what they were doing.

I found all of that and more in Susan and the White Pony preschool that she directed. The "more" (which I didn't have words for at the time) was what this book is all about. It is what I call "heart" and what she calls "the big picture" or "intuition."

Susan knows the literature. You'll find many examples of the depth of her knowledge within the pages of this book. But the value of what this book brings forth is not just the wonderful research and valuable parenting strategies. It is what Susan has learned from a lifetime of listening, observing, and trusting the process. Susan knows that growth and learning inevitably include periods of equilibrium followed by periods of disequilibrium. Life without discomfort is life without growth. I thought of one of my favorite songs, "Anthem" by Leonard Cohen, as I read this book:

> *... Ring the bells that still can ring Forget your*
> *perfect offering There is a crack, a crack in*
> *everything That's how the light gets in...*

I hope that as you read this book, you begin to recognize your own inner wisdom and to trust that with your loving support and encouragement, the children in your care will come to see "the cracks" or the painful experiences they have, or will inevitably have, while growing up, as gifts…aids to their growth and maturity as well as their compassion and capacity to move forward during difficult times courageously.

May we all learn to welcome those periods of disequilibrium and to trust in our ability to tune into our own inner wisdom as Susan has learned to do. This book will surely help us all along the way!

Table of Contents

Chapter One: Focus on the Big Picture

"What I wish I had known and understood is this: most of what we think is important doesn't matter. Much of what we worry about is irrelevant. We sweat the small stuff to such an enormous degree. We worry about the minutiae when we should be focusing on the big picture."

Anonymous

Dear Reader,

This book is a love letter to you. You may be a mother so immersed in the daily minutiae of your life that you miss out on the dazzling overview of all you do. If you are like most women, I wonder how often you pause long enough to feel compassion for your oversized expectations for yourself. Maybe you're a new mom or a woman trying to decide whether to get pregnant or adopt a child and have a hundred "What if?" questions. On the other hand, I fully understand your anxiety if you are a mother who is finding child's behavior impossible or a grandmother looking for new insights into her grandchildren's challenges.

As a human development consultant, a mother, and a grandmother, I know that you worry and, crazy as it may sound, even feel guilty for things you don't know. It's one of the complex, unforgiving ideas we have of being a mother today. Who among us can ever live up to our own idealized images of motherhood? As psychotherapist and author Dr. Harriet Lerner says, "It's a job description so idealized that none of us can fill it."

Our complex legacies

As women, we inherit legacies of what it means to be a mother. These include incalculable love and lofty intentions, as well as misalignments, missed opportunities, losses and trauma. I've learned to be grateful for the forethought of my ancestors and the awareness that their traumas played a role in shaping my childhood and my mothering. In the next chapter, I reveal my own psychological/spiritual family tree along with a lifequake that catapulted me into a period of incessant worry about my children. I didn't even start shoring up my personhood, separate from my role as a mother, until I was 42, when I was graced with a vision of the trajectory of my life. If you already know you're a person as well as a mother, you're way ahead of where I was then.

I've been in love with mothers and their abilities to self-reflect and manifest change since my career working with them began forty years ago. I documented their stories in *The Inner Parent,* written with my co-author, Marti Keller. Marti and I saw that our culture blames mothers for everything and conditions them to criticize themselves if they or their children ever encounter problems. Yet, despite these tendencies toward guilt and self-blame, we witnessed that mothers were the ones who often found amazing, internal and external resources and brought about real change that was beneficial to everyone.

Our view at the time was that mothers have always been the ones ushering in a more compassionate world, and our book, *The Inner Parent,* contained countless glimpses into parents' lives that readers still find inspiring.

Later, in my book, *The Best Things Parents Do*, I shared stories from real parents who came into my life as a parent consultant. Readers tell me they still find the book's insights and practical strategies helpful. However, I feel passionately that today in the upheaval of modern life, mothers need a wider lens to empower themselves to prioritize and protect their own well-being. The last two decades have ushered in unprecedented change. It sounds like a cliché to say the world is a different place today, but for parents it's demonstrably true, and it's easy to lose our bearings.

Decades of change

The internet has transformed communication about child-rearing, giving us the abilities to network and share information in ways we couldn't have previously imagined. At the same time, social media stresses us by providing more opportunities to compare ourselves with others and question our own judgment. We have also lived through a pandemic that offered glimpses of more humanitarian attitudes toward work/life balance, but the post-pandemic reality is that women with mid to upper- level jobs have significant rates of burnout as a result of prioritizing everyone else's needs at home and at work.

In addition, family configurations have morphed into new shapes, on the one hand, freeing us to value the countless ways people can provide loving support for children, but also making it clear how desperately we need to commit to meeting the needs of all families. Where do we turn to get mothers and children the support they need? From my perspective as a developmental consultant, the fields of anthropology and social biology provide clues about how our distant past can inform our future by awakening us to our proven capacities to nurture and tend to one another.

The Evolution of Motherhood

I am fascinated by the work of the social anthropologist, Professor Emerita Sarah Blather Hrdy, She has highlighted the evolutionary history of women sharing in the care of each other's children and supporting one another through challenges. She urges us to look at our evolutionary history as a key to envisioning a future when child-rearing becomes more communal, with community-based peer support for women and policy changes that encourage men to play their parenting roles more fully. As my colleague, Dr. Lillian Katz famously said, "I really believe that each of us must come to care about other people's children. We must awaken to the reality that the welfare of our children and grandchildren is intimately linked to the welfare of other people's children."

As a constant collector of women's stories, I am convinced that authentic narratives activate our moral compass and reveal the ways evolution is already leading us into more caring community. The stories show again and again that it's tuning into our inner knowing rather than heeding the prescriptions for what mothering should be, that move us forward. The true-life tales in this book illustrate the best things mothers do to help us create a more matricentric future when caregiving and consensus-building are the norm and women are empowered to respond to challenges in ways that change society as a whole and embrace everyone's needs.

My own life in the past two decades has included the joy of creating a compassion symposium at my school featuring a keynote address by the late Dr. Carol Weyland Conner, the founder of groundbreaking programs for the underserved. Dr. Conner always acted with the big picture of "all of us taking care of all of us" in mind. But each of us also has the ability to take a panoramic view of our own lives and make choices that move ourselves, our children, and the world forward towards a more compassionate perspective. To feel more compassion towards ourselves and others, we often need to step out of our habitual reactivity and into the wisdom provided by thinking in terms of a bigger picture.

Big picture parenting

What does big picture thinking even mean? In the world of business, we're familiar with the idea that those who want to succeed have to aspire to big picture thinking. In other words, to advance, they must keep their eyes on the prize and avoid getting lost in the minutiae. Mothers are not competing to climb the success ladder, at least not in their own homes. So, if that is the case, then how is focusing on the big picture relevant to their lives or yours? What might pausing to think in a more expansive way do for you?

As a start, thinking about the big picture can allow you to take in the enormity of all that you do. Our preoccupation with the endless details of daily life almost always obscures our self-perceptions. No matter what a great job you're doing as a mother, you still have to deal with the entire mental load of keeping track of endless tasks and priorities. And, I know no matter how much you do, it never feels like enough. It's your unrelenting inner voices that leave you feeling anxious or guilty. Sadly, mothers who strive for perfection at work and at home often experience burnout without even realizing it.

So, in this book, I use the term" big picture thinking" to describe seeing yourself, your child, or a situation from a broader perspective. I have seen again and again that kind of reflection is the doorway out of unproductive anxiety, guilt, and overdoing. Thinking in the big picture helps us to assess our real priorities, to understand the context of a situation, and incorporate other points of view. Most importantly, it allows us to engage in the mindfulness practice of observing our own thoughts and feelings.

In reality, much of what we routinely tell ourselves is not logical at all and leaves us stuck. For example, we can get mired in the details of something that appears to be going wrong with our child leaving us unable to see the bigger context. This recycling of unproductive thoughts is what psychologist Dr. Ethan Kross describes as "chatter" in his bestselling book by the same name. Chatter is the critical voice in our head that comments on everything we do, think, and feel. To ensure our survival, however, our brains have a negative bias, hardwired to give more weight to negative experiences.

When we're upset about a challenge, stress can propel us into repetitive discouraging thoughts like "I can't believe this is happening." "This isn't real." Thought patterns sometimes become deeply grooved in our neural pathways, causing us to get stuck in those loops and interpret them as reality. That's called rumination, and we all do it. It is the way our brain's work to ensure our survival. However, Kross offers us a way out.

The benefits of a wider lens

He has focused his career on big picture thinking, or what psychologists call construal theory, the ability to mentally distance from an object, event, or from spiraling negative thoughts. This concept is illustrated in the popular phrase "seeing the forest for the trees." Kross describes the advantage of being able to" zoom out" of everyday rumination to have an overview of what's important. He says, "The mind is flexible if we know how to bend it." If I'm locked in a power struggle with my child, it can help if I pause and remember that what matters most to me is staying emotionally connected. That requires me to take some mental space for reflection. Another term for that is accessing the big picture, and the process has roots that go back through time.

Although big-picture thinking is a relatively new psychological term, it's an age-old concept in both Eastern and Western religious traditions. As Thich Nhat Hanh says,

> *Until you change your thinking, you will always recycle your experience.*

For example, prayer and meditation are ancient avenues for lifting out of what religious traditions call constant ruminations of "the lower mind," to have more expansive perspectives, what some people might even call viewing the world the way God might see it. Dr. Kross grew up with a father who constantly shared his explorations of Eastern religions, and Kross admits that his dad's immersion in spiritual thought influenced his own interest in big-picture thinking.

Kross notes that most of us don't even realize when we engage in big-picture thinking, and he urges us to become aware of the freedom it can provide us. You have probably had times when you stepped out of a storm of self-critique during a difficult situation and suddenly saw an overview full of possibility. Those times are sometimes called "aha" experiences and science has revealed that our brains can be reshaped during those moments. It's like turning your TV to a different channel. *Oprah Magazine* columnist and life coach, Martha Beck, says,

"When we tune into the big picture of what really matters to us and make decisions to create the life we want, that's when the miracles start happening"

Thankfully, we live in an age when breakthrough thinking and mutual support for it are recognized as pathways forward.

I witness mothers taking time to try to think in big picture ways during difficult situations every day, and it often transforms their point of view. They ask questions like, "Does this really matter?" "What positive ways could I approach this?". Believing that we can access inner and outer resources fuels our confidence that we can handle challenges as individuals and as a society. However, equipping ourselves to respond wisely to the complexities of life isn't always a popular pastime.

The transformative nature of challenge

Parents are often urged to believe that the best way to inoculate themselves against troubling problems is to align themselves with the latest parenting philosophy. This book takes a unique perspective. It starts from the supposition that there will be challenges, losses, and even "lifequakes" along the motherhood journey, and when that happens, we need to tap into inner and outer resources so we can handle our dilemmas in self-nurturing ways. I'm grateful to the bestselling author, Bruce Feiler for normalizing the reality that life is full of disruptions, and we can best understand how to manage them through the holistic view provided by a wider lens.

In his bestselling book, *Life Is in the Transitions,* Feiler points out that most of us experience three to five major upheavals or lifequakes during a lifetime, not to mention smaller "disruptions" that occur every twelve to eighteen months. His book offers compelling stories of people convinced that their lives have been ruined then miraculously seeing a bigger picture. Feiler claims that modern life requires people to get good at going through huge changes. His book is full of real-life tales demonstrating the surprising ways people face disorienting dilemmas, give up dysfunctional beliefs, and reinvent their perspectives and their lives for all of us to see. They are the creative problem-solvers of our time who go through hard learning and show us how to ride the waves of change like graceful surfers.

So, rather than looking for the latest trend that promises to make your life perfect, believe in your ability to tap into your own knowing, especially in times of crisis.

Actually, in my experience the most significant parenting miracles occur when mothers go through disruptions to their best-laid plans even though at the time the events may trigger mountainous amounts of worry. The idea that we can do mothering perfectly or that we should feel guilty about worrying sabotages our mental health. From my professional experience I see that anxiety can provide us with the energy and motivation to think from new perspectives. One way or another, we all acknowledge that humans have the greatest opportunities to grow when life seems the hardest. Those are the times when our habitual view of ourselves can feel worn out, and we stop to ask "Who am I?" Ultimately, real awakenings often begin when we have no idea how to get out of our spiraling, self-defeating thoughts. The normal rumination of the human brain creates tracks of worry, and stepping into a big picture perspective like "What's the most important aspect of this situation in the long run?" forces us to look beyond our limited thinking.

After decades of working with mothers and from my own mothering experience, I'm aware of recurring themes that can keep us up at night. For example, you may be worrying about so-called milestones because your child isn't getting potty trained or learning to read according to some arbitrary schedule. And I know, dear reader, you can get lost in pain and self-blame when your child is having a problem with a friend, and you don't know how to help. When it comes to parenting challenges, it's easy to leave compassion for yourself out of the equation. I also understand you can feel guilty when your child needs you, and you're stuck at work, and you feel bad about work left undone when you need to be at home. I see how exhausted and burned out you can get trying to respond to everyone's expectations.

Yet again and again, I feel privileged to spend time with mothers facing challenges in self-reflective ways by examining why they are feeling stuck and seeing creative ways to move forward. That's why I want to remind women to ponder society's unrealistic job descriptions for mothers. Pausing for big-picture thinking can free them to see themselves and their children in a more compassionate way. How do we go about taking those restorative breaks when our thoughts are spiraling?

Access to big-picture thinking

Ethan Kross and other psychologists offer suggestions to help us when we have a problem and our mind is stuck in analyzing competing priorities. Here are their ideas for accessing big-picture thinking:

- Stop to breathe and ground ourselves in the moment.
- Journal about our feelings.
- Make our self-talk more positive.
- Mentally time-travel into the past or future.
- Use positive affirmations to program our minds in helpful ways.
- List everything in our lives that makes us feel grateful.
- Or my personal favorite collaborating with someone to see things in a big-picture way instead of just venting.

However, dear reader. we can't leap into big-picture thinking through a "to do" list. True big-picture thinking comes from gently stepping back from a situation in order to see all the parts involved. And guess what? When we take time to take a bird's eye view of our lives, we often access previously unacknowledged sources of wisdom. The other name for those inspirations that allow us to suddenly recognize patterns or connect the dots of information is intuition.

Essentially, the stories in this book are unique and authentic because they reflect the intuitive processes of real people. The people involved might not have called their insights or decision-making intuition when they occurred. That raises the question, "How can we recognize or understand intuitive thinking if it's not part of our everyday perspectives or the way we learned decision-making works?"

In common parlance, we often refer to intuition as a gut feeling or sixth sense. *The British Journal of Psychology* has defined it as what happens when the brain draws on past experiences and external cues to make a decision, but it happens quite unconsciously. Research at the HeartMath Institute sees the seat of intuition as the heart, and their fascinating research suggests that the heart is a highly intelligent sensory organ that receives and processes intuitive information even before the brain does. Although the institute's scientific findings are new, spiritual figures throughout the ages have concurred with them and pointed to the heart as the source of intuition.

The origin of intuition

As an example, the Indian spiritual master, Meher Baba, said that intuition, stemming from the heart, is not an emotion or psychic thing and it's not imagination. He said it develops a higher contact with reality than reason does. You may already be aware that we are living in a most unique period spiritually. In his book, *The Discourses,* Meher Baba observes that the huge shift in consciousness that occurred millennia ago was from instinct to reason, and the evolutionary shift happening now is from reason to intuition.

The evolution from reason to intuition

My experiences as a consultant lead me to believe that the idea of an evolutionary shift from reason to intuition has special significance for mothers. In her *Psychology Today* article, "The Neuroscience of Women's Intuition," Dr. Judith Orloff explores the important role of intuition in women's lives. Women are more apt to utilize intuitive processes when they are making important decisions in life, as we will explore in this book's last chapter. That doesn't mean that they ignore facts or reason, or that they are diminished by the old patriarchal discrediting of "women's intuition" as having no place in the bigger arenas of power. Men have intuitive knowing too, and knowledge of these faculties can help all of us become better collaborators.

Let's start by exploring the intuitive knowing that comes through the stories in this book. How do people experience intuition? Although it is often dryly described as an unconscious processing of information leading to quick judgments, in lived experience it can feel like a strike of lightning. At other times, it seeps into awareness more gradually.

Later you will hear about Darla and how at the age of 60 she was suddenly seized with the certainty that she had to foster a child or Hannah who realized during an emergency surgery to save her unborn daughter that she had to radically change her life. A vision of an unexpected life-change also occurred to Pema Chodron. After an event that shattered her identity, she intuited that although she was a single parent with two teenagers living at home, she wanted to become a Tibetan Buddhist nun. However, not all of the stories are about people making huge alterations in their lives. Most of them are about facing practical parenting challenges and lifequakes with creativity and resourcefulness.

Through the ages, our best learning often comes through stories and the honest, often surprising narratives collected here are bound to open hearts. We are too often unaware of the courageous struggles of mothers who often go through so much without receiving needed support from others. They are the real heroes of our time. Their stories inspire us with the reality that big picture thinking lifted them out of self-defeating patterns as they struggled to understand their circumstances from fresh perspectives. No matter what the problem or the crisis, the miracles occurred when they opened themselves to an innovative lens of new knowing.

Ultimately, I believe stories like these are the teaching-tales of our time. Shining light on the resilience and compassion of mothers benefits us all. Each chapter explores a topic that involves real challenges in mothers' lives.

- Chapter Two explores our legacies and how reflecting on them helps us to move forward in our own evolution.

- Chapter Three asks questions about how we can create a shared vision of pregnancy, birth, and parenthood and promote well-being for all women and families.

- Chapter Four, grounds us in the pressing need for us all to become more empathic and skilled collaborators to support each other in this constantly changing society.

- Chapter Five explores the historic shame mothers experience when their children's behavior is judged as out-of-control and offers amazing strategies for efficacy and transformation.

- Chapter Six introduces the important roles mothers play in building their children's social skills and resolving problems of bullying and exclusion.

- Chapter Seven revisits a question posed throughout the book, "How do we know children?" and zeroes in on the necessity to reframe society's view that children have to continually compete in order to win success.

- Chapter Eight looks at the history of silence regarding women's health issues and the liberating empowerment of women claiming the right to share their own stories.

- Chapter Nine discusses the process of making critical decisions and introduces the idea that the choices we make ripple through the lives of others. To make that point, it examines the life-changing decisions made by three women who have ushered in change in our society: Maya Angelou, Pema Chodron, and Brené Brown.

Although *The Best Things Mothers Do* highlights recurring themes in our growth and learning, the stories are not always organized in a linear way. There are tales about the transition to motherhood in almost every chapter, and Chapter Seven, which champions the ability to value a child in the current moment, actually begins with adolescents, goes back to our expectations for infants, and moves forward again to the often-overwhelming stresses of teenagers.

Most importantly, the through line of all the narratives is the ability to look at the big picture with a focus on growth. The book doesn't promise picture-book outcomes in child-rearing. In fact, in the very last story, Ann Lamott is faced with the challenge of letting her beloved adult son do his own learning while she learns to embrace and care for herself. *The Best Things Mothers Do* invites us to accept the messiness of life that isn't perfect but helps us make choices that bring more meaning to our lives.

The title of each story represents an example of the best thing mothers do.

Most of the stories came to me through interviews that women have so generously shared. Sometimes, I have given the parents fictional names to protect their identities, or when they were willing to identify themselves, I often use only their first names. In addition, I've collected many stories through reading interviews, articles, and memoirs. That's why you may find that some of the names like Glennon Doyle, Serena Williams, Julia Roberts, Naomi Osaka, or even Betty Ford, may be familiar to you.

In the next chapter, dear reader, I invite you to explore your legacy in all its complexity, joy, pain, and opportunities for growth. My introductory story opens the chapter when I express gratitude to my birth grandmother and reveal a lifequake that propelled me into a new understanding of motherhood and the desire to write this book. It is coupled with four shorter but extraordinary real-life stories about the power of our abilities to learn from our ancestors but also to find our own way.

Reflective questions:

What is your vision of motherhood?

Have you ever had a fantasy baby or child who lives in your imagination?

If you are a mother, how does the fantasy compare with reality?

What do you tell yourself about the rewards and challenges of parenthood?

Resources:

Aiyana, Sheleana interviewing Harriet Lerner, PhD, July 16, 2020, "Navigating Difficult Mother/ Daughter Relationships," *https://youtube/Kv9_Jx13Iu4*

Meher Baba, 2007, *Discourses,* Sheriar Foundation, sixth edition.

Childre, Lew Doc, Martin, Howard, Beech, Donna, *The HeartMath Solution: The Institute of HeartMath's Revolutionary Program for Enjoying the Heart's Intelligence, Harper,* 2011.

Feiler, Bruce, *Life is in the Transitions,* Penguin, 2021.

Katz, Lillian, *The Developing Child,* Exchange Press, 4, 25,2002.

Gilbert, Elizabeth, "Magic Lessons", podcast, Episode 208, 9,6, 2018. *Leap into the Fire,* featuring *Marsha Beck,*

Hanh, Thich Nhat, *Being Peace,* Parallax Press, 1987.

Kross, Ethan, PhD, *Chatter: The Voice in Our Head and Why It Matters,* Crown Publishers, 2021.

Pearsall, Paul, *The Heart's Code,* Harmony, 1999.

Pema Chodron, Oprah, "Oprah Talks to Pema Chodren," online interview, October 20, 2019.

Orloff, Judy, MD, "The Neuroscience of Women's Intuition," *Psychology Today, Aug 12, 2024.*

Silvestri, Kenneth PhD, *A Wider Lens; How to See Your Life Differently,* Bookbaby, 2018.

Chapter Two: The Big Picture of Discovering Your Family Heritage

Edward Sellner

Discoveries of the past

What gifts did your ancestors give you? Supermodel Chrissy Teigen had tears in her eyes when she learned on PBS's *Finding Your Roots* that both her great-grandparents worked in Thailand's rice fields every day. "They had to constantly bend over picking the rice, grain by grain," she said with awe. She was also visibly moved when the show's host, Henry Gates Jr., showed her a photo of her maternal grandmother's food cart and told her that she went out twice a day to sell home-cooked dishes to neighbors in their small Thai village. When Gates asked Tiegen how she felt hearing those facts about her Thai ancestors, she spoke wistfully, "I guess you would expect me to say that their lives are so different than mine. But I don't feel that. I'm struck by how similar we are."

Tiegen went on to describe her passion for food. She is the author of two cookbooks and loves nothing more than cooking for her husband, singer John Legend, and four young children. "Food is the constant in my life that never lets me down. There is nothing I love more than being the one to serve a new food to one of my kids and to watch their reactions. Tiegen feels her love and appreciation for food was her ancestors' gift to her.

Over the last two decades, *Finding Your Roots*, a show that explores the ancestry of celebrities in many different fields, has become a phenomenon with an estimated sixteen million viewers. Its popularity reflects America's newfound passion for acquiring information about ancestry. In preparation for every episode, genealogical detectives work behind the scenes to answer questions guests may have had for years. Sometimes, hearing an ancestor's life decisions can be disheartening-a mother who abandoned her children or a great, great-grandparent who owned slaves. Occasionally, guests discover a famous family member. More often, however, the research highlights courageous stories of ordinary people, like Teigen's grandmother, who handled hardships with resilience and sometimes made bold decisions that changed their family tree.

Tiegen's appreciative reactions to her grandparents and great-grandparents weren't unusual. Guests on the show often say that their ancestors' stories connect in subtle ways to their own. Their experience offers us all a glimpse that we aren't separate from those who have gone before us. It also becomes apparent that each person on the family tree, going back generations, had their own story. This may propel the guest celebrity to reflect on the fact that their own life has a trajectory, a narrative that may inspire someone who comes after them in the future. At the program's conclusion, Gates presents each guest with a genealogical summary of their ancestry called *The Book of Life.*

Viewers might imagine what their *Book of Life* would look like. Perhaps, you have constructed your own version from your genealogical investigations. You might wonder where to start.

Intergenerational inspiration

What were the influences on your ancestors' lives? How would you characterize their relationships? Learning about the past may reveal patterns of trauma or abuse, and that information can help you make needed changes in your life. That's what happened when bestselling author, Brene Brown discovered patterns of alcoholism, which we will explore in Chapter Nine. Her story shows that family stories can aid our understanding of current problems, especially when they spur us to get curious about our own parents' upbringing and the pressures they felt growing up. Sometimes, our reflection helps us see that our spiritual beliefs diverge from our family's, though we may remain close to them.

On the other hand, since motherhood can involve disruptions in our best-laid plans, hearing about our ancestors' struggles can reassure us that we are not alone. We may discover decisions our ancestors made that resulted in our lives being better. Research shows that thinking about our ancestors can motivate us to persevere and feel confident in the face of challenges. It can help us walk a mile in their shoes. What do you think your ancestors felt about events in their lives? What helped them to see the big picture when they were making important decisions?

Thinking in terms of the emotional/spiritual aspects of our ancestry can help us create a different kind of family tree that goes beyond a list of names and dates. In a Psychology Today article called, "Who do you think you are? Clues from your family of origin," psychotherapist Kenneth Silvestri recommends creating a genogram, a graphic representation which includes stories, themes, and people's relationships.

I am interested in your story, dear reader, and I'm hoping that reading the narratives of the brave women in this chapter (a couple of them were my ancestors) will inspire you to explore the big picture of your family. What were the stories you heard as a child? Research shows that intergenerational stories can play a significant role in the lives of young people. We can start telling family stories to our children at an early age. Studies also reveal that the ability to pass on family stories has particular importance for mothers as imparters of history to their children.

Stories of generational strengths

For over twenty years, professors Robyn Fivush and Marshall Duke of Emory University have studied the impact of intergenerational stories on self-esteem and feelings of empowerment in youth. Their many research projects have shown that hearing how previous generations handled tough times is a foundation for the development of confidence in young people. When we teach children that their grandparents and great-grandparents survived challenges resiliently, they gain confidence in their own abilities to handle change.

Fivush and Duke created the Family Narratives Lab at Emory University, which examines how children, adults, and families tell the stories of their past, both the good times and the bad, and how the stories are related to their psychological health. The stories in this book often reflect transformations in mothers' lives and the narratives they are creating.

Strategies for discovering and sharing your family stories:

- Make storytelling a regular activity at family gatherings.
- Learn how to ask questions that get people talking.
- Know your purpose, the kinds of stories you are trying to hear.
- Ask about the hard times as well as the happy ones.
- Look for stories of bravery and resilience in the face of challenge.
- Ask about connections between people and relations that were disconnected.
- Use photos to get people talking about past experiences.
- Be prepared to write or record stories that can be shared in the future.
- Get more information about family legends.
- Explore the origin of family traditions and rituals.
- Try to understand what family patterns you want to leave behind and those you want to continue.

Reflective questions:

Do you remember family stories from your childhood?

Were there core values passed on from generation to generation?

Are there patterns you want to leave behind?

Resources:

British Psychological Society, "The Benefits of Thinking about our Ancestors", December 2010.

Fivush, Robyn, PhD, "Remembering and Reminiscing: How Individual Lives Are Constructed in Family Narratives," Memory Studies, 2008.

Fivush, Robyn, PhD," Intergenerational Narratives and Identity Across Development," Developmental Review, 2016.

Galindo, Israel, Boomer, Elaine, Reagan, Don, A *Family Genogram Workbook,* Galindo Publishers, January 2017.

Fivush, Robyn, PhD, "Creating Hope Through Future Selves; How Hope for Our Future Selves Facilitates Meaning in life," Psychology Today blog, 2025.

Silvestri, Kenneth, EdD, "Who Do You Think You Are? Clues from Your Family of Origin," Psychology Today, June, 2019.

Here are the stories:

The true-life stories that follow illustrate the surprising ways four very different women reflect on their emotional/spiritual inheritance. I hope this helps you, dear reader, to explore your legacy and gives you greater clarity about your identity as a mother and as a person.

The first is my own inter-generational story and how looking at the challenges in my maternal family line made me feel more compassionate towards my mother and deeply grateful for both her birth and biological moms. I met my birth grandmother in a dream while writing her story. Furthermore, writing their stories made me more empathetic with the mothers I consult with every day in my profession.

In the second story, we hear Lauren Williams' touching narrative of her Aunt Betty's pivotal role in 9/11. It invites us to see how a tragic loss can super-charge a family's identity and empower them to move forward in remarkable ways. Aunt Betty is still alive in the life of Lauren's little girl, Olivia, who never met her aunt, but she talks about her often.

In the third story, we travel with Jodie Patterson on her life-changing pilgrimage to her southern family home. Jodie draws energy from African American ancestors that convinces her she can handle what feels like insurmountable dilemmas in her own life.

In the fourth story, we see the evolution of our beliefs and the process of forming our own identities. Coleen loved the spiritual foundation her parents gave her growing up, but when she had to make hard decisions about the birth of her unborn baby, she learned the power of being able to disagree with her family and still love them.

In the fifth story, Glennon Doyle marvels at her mother's flexibility in supporting her through many dramatic metamorphoses in her identity, all in the public eye. She credits her mother's unwavering, accepting love as the steady force helping her through all her changes, and in her own mother's devotion to her grandmother, she sees an inspiring matrilineal tree of support.

We can look at the process of seeing our connections to our ancestors as strength-based archeology, allowing us to dig deep to discover resources we never knew we had and understand the new directions that we want our lives to take.

Best Thing: Create an Emotional-Spiritual Family Tree

Chinese proverb

We don't become mothers the moment we conceive or meet the child we're going to foster or adopt. I believe the process begins generations before we were born.

I think a lot about one of my ancestors, my birth grandmother, Mary Nicholson, who was a mother for only seven weeks before she died of "childbed fever." However, in the short time available to her, she made courageous decisions that affected our family for generations.

I can trace my journey as a mother, with all its psychological and spiritual threads, back to the day and hour Mary gave birth to my mother and named her Jane, a name meaning God is gracious.

I picture her holding my mom for the first time and imagine her fantasies of taking my mom to the park for the first time, walking her to school, and a lifetime of shared experiences.

Signs of trouble

It would have taken several days for Mary to realize that something was wrong, not with her baby but with her own body. The beginning signs of sepsis, the infection still responsible for most maternal deaths today from childbirth, can come as a foul-smelling discharge which escalates into a fever. Ironically, Mary was the first in her family to give birth in a hospital, but it was probably bacteria from the delivery room that resulted in her death.

It must have been awkward for Mary to talk about her symptoms with the doctor. Growing up in a devout Irish Catholic family, with a sister who was already a nun, she would have been extremely modest.

As time went on, it became apparent that the family's prayers for Mary to live were not going to be realized. Mary probably felt guilty that she was dying. I can't imagine her grief at having to leave her newborn daughter. Now, in the big picture, she wondered if she could provide Jane with a home where she would always be appreciated and honored for her unique self.

Big Picture of the future

After hearing his wife was going to die, Mary's husband, Walter, abdicated responsibility for raising his new daughter. It seemed like too much. On the other hand, Mary's parents would have insisted that they would raise Jane, since they had other young children at home. Finally, instead of worrying about what everyone else thought was best for her baby, Mary thought deeply about what mattered to her. She knew she didn't want Jane to be raised as another mouth to feed in her family home. She wanted her daughter to be surrounded by love and she thought about her sister Catherine. She was a year older than Mary and the kindest and most compassionate person in their big Irish family. She was flourishing in another state with her husband, Robert, but Mary dared to write and ask her to make a life-altering decision.

Mary's letter to Catherine was a way of offering a prayer to the universe. She asked her sister if she would leave her new life and become a loving mother to her baby. Catherine surprised everyone by answering "yes," that she and Robert would move back to San Francisco and adopt Jane. So that's how my adored grandmother, Catherine, the most constant source of unconditional love and nurturance during my childhood, entered motherhood, by surprise, not by design.

These are the untold stories so common in women's lives throughout history.

Tentative beginnings

Thinking of the challenges my grandmother faced during her transition to motherhood tugs at my heart. Catherine was grieving the loss of her vibrant, younger sister, Mary, at a time when psychological grief was little understood. She may well have experienced survivor's guilt about being the one alive to mother my mom.

Catherine's loving nature turned out to be a lifesaver for my mom, who was a highly sensitive baby and child. As she got older, she had nervous habits and panic attacks. There were few child-rearing books available to mothers, and certainly none that would offer insight into my mother's sensitivity. I think my mom suffered from a condition described by Nancy Verrier in her 1993 book about adoption called *The Primal Wound*. The premise of Verrier's book is that an infant experiences trauma when separated from the biological mother at birth. For nine months, my mother had lived inside my birth grandmother, Mary Nicholson's body, listening to her voice and sensing her emotions. She had also been held and comforted by Mary for about a month after her birth. However, the knowledge that her new baby had experienced trauma didn't exist when Catherine was a new mom.

Catherine's newly configured family went through many hardships. Moving back to California was a financial challenge for her and Robert. They struggled through the depression, and Catherine went to work as a nurse when Robert couldn't find work. Nevertheless, my mother led a very sheltered life, going to church weekly and attending Catholic schools.

Then, at the age of 18, she was thrust into a whole new world of adult responsibilities when she met my father right after high school, and they married.

My mother's transition to adulthood

From my mom's own report, leaving home and setting up her own household was a huge step forward in independence. My father was nine years older, and as a merchant marine, he was away for months at a time. Soon, there was another leap forward when she learned she was going to become a mother.

It must have taken great bravery for my mom to have her first baby, me, in the same hospital where her mother had given birth to her. My mom was a tentative new mother who read and absorbed all the advice in the childcare books by the expert of the day, Dr. Benjamin Spock. However, she also possessed many of the beautiful, generous qualities of her adopted mother, Catherine.

We lived in the country when I was young, and for months there would be just two of us while my dad was out to sea. We loved making bouquets of wildflowers from the hillside and taking care of our chickens. My mom read to me from an early age, and we loved the poetry of Wordsworth and Longfellow. She told me stories of the saints that left luminous impressions in my mind that still exist today. She would also confide in me and ask me for advice about problems. Later, my brother and sister brought welcome sibling relationships into our home. However, in that halcyon setting, that still feels so nurturing in my memory, I was unconsciously parenting my own mother. I feel blessed to understand now how that propelled me into my future career.

Now I realize that as an adult; I studied human development on some level to unravel the mysteries of my beloved mom's early life. Since I had been like a mother to my mom, it seemed natural to become a parent educator and preschool director at the age of twenty-one. Before I was a mother, my career took off in countless satisfying ways. I eventually enjoyed consulting with parents in diverse cultural communities across several states and becoming a college instructor and author. But my main fulfillment in life came after we had kids. My husband and I had three children and took joy in their growth and activities. Then, at the age of forty-two, my work and my life, as I knew them, were suddenly interrupted.

My life plan disrupted by divorce

My husband and I separated abruptly and started filing for divorce. Up to that point, I had been living my own vision of idealized motherhood, working part-time, and immersing myself in a caring community of families with similar values. I realize now that my personal identity had been focused on being a good mom, someone who wanted to give her children a perfect life.

The unexpected separation shocked our children. Previously, when they had heard of other families divorcing, they got upset and asked if it would ever happen to us. I reassured them that our family was surrounded by a "magic circle." In retrospect, I realize this was ill-advised, but I had never imagined divorce in our future. Today, I see my reference to the 'magic circle" as a way of enshrining the nuclear family, the American ideal. However, now our family was no longer going to be nuclear, and I didn't know what shape it would take.

In the first few weeks, my linear life and sense of self got turned upside down. In his bestselling book, *Life is in the Transitions,* Bruce Feiler describes this sudden transition as a "lifequake" that forces a person to think in a big picture way and reorients their ways of seeing the world with an intensity beyond their control.

I had been proud of being a mother who could work part-time so I could devote myself to my children. Now, when I had to scramble to find a full-time job, I was inspired by remembering that my grandmother, Catherine had bravely gone to work when her husband couldn't. She was my role model.

Surprising realms of reflection

That didn't mean I didn't worry. My mind was obsessed with "What if?" questions about how these abrupt changes would affect my children's future. Worrying about them was like an emotional roller coaster. But then life itself nudged me into seeing the big picture.

I must have asked the universe if this surprise detour in my planned existence would be permanent because that's when I had a life-changing experience.

It happened suddenly one night, when I woke up to a luminous picture of my whole life spread out before me, like a fuzzy map. A voice inside said, "What you're going through now will be a small part of your life journey." For a second, my reaction was, "You must be kidding. That can't be." However, I was enveloped in a force of love and acceptance so completely, I couldn't do anything but absorb it. I was humbled by seeing the big picture when I didn't have the mental distance to imagine a positive future for myself or my children. The vision also allowed me to let go of the illusion that I could control my children's lives. I could see they were going to be fine.

I am reminded of a poem by Julian of Norwich:

All shall be well.

And all shall be well.

And all matter of things shall be well.

For there is a force of love

Moving through the universe

That holds us fast and never lets us go.

My visit from unconditional love reshaped my life in profound ways and pointed me toward healing. Since childhood, I had purposely pushed my own needs and individuation aside to invest in the well-being of others – first my mother, then my husband, then joyfully and appropriately my children. In response, a friend offered me an unorthodox idea. She suggested I go to Codependents Anonymous, not because my ex-husband was an alcoholic (he wasn't) but because I had to learn to focus on what mattered to me.

It took courage to attend my first meeting. The people, the guidelines, and the protocols were all foreign to me. However, the principles of paying attention to one's own needs rather than trying to solve the problems of others made so much sense. I still love the premises of the recovery movement.

Step-parenting with love

Five years after my divorce, I married Jeff, a wonderful man, and my life fully bloomed with happiness. He was the perfect stepfather, someone I could fully partner with, but by then, my perspective on motherhood had changed. I no longer viewed my role as a "good mother" as someone responsible for everything in my children's lives. I had seen in my nighttime vision that they had their own destinies. I felt compassion for my previous self, who felt so responsible for everything.

Losing my "good mother" identity made me more compassionate with myself and with those parents I counseled about their parenting struggles. Was I a good mom when my kids had accomplishments, and bad when my kids were having a hard time? Or was I the same person trying to support them in their individual journeys, the best that I could? In being forced out of my good mother persona, however, I felt a kinship with all mothers.

To conclude this reflection on my journey as a mother, I offer a quote from the book, *Matricentric Feminism* by Andrea O'Reilly: "The term mother and mothering refer to any individual who engages in mothering and includes anyone who takes up the work of mothering as a central activity in their life."

In my family tree, I consider my birth grandmother, Mary Nicholson, to be one of my mothers, as was my adopted grandmother, Catherine, who nurtured three generations: my mother, me, my siblings, and my children. As she got older, my mother showed tremendous strength as she supported me and my children through divorce and beyond. Later, she shocked us all by going back to college and becoming a prison minister.

I realize now that the real magic circle hadn't been my nuclear family of my husband and our two children. It was my matrilineal line that gave me strength, the role models of women who could face adversity with courage, have faith that the force of love was supporting them, and shape their destinies.

Our mothers and their complex lives

Dear reader, the story of your mothering heritage may have less drama than mine did. However, I'm sure, as with any human being, your history has many elements, and I hope you will be tender with yourself as you explore it. I wonder with compassion about the mothering you received. I'm curious about your mother and her mother, and about the precepts and expectations that were passed down through the generations about being a mom in your family.

These are the emotional/ spiritual foundations of your story. Tuning into the big picture can help you create a narrative of your life that you can share with others, including your children.

Reflective questions:

Have you ever had moments when you glimpsed the big picture of your life?

Resources:

McGoldrick, Monica, *The Genogram Journey: Reconnecting with Your Family*, Norton, 2011.

O" Reilly, Andrea, *Matricentric Feminism: Theory, Activism, Practice*, Demeter Press, 2021.

Best Thing: Believe in the Power of One Person

"One person can make a difference, and everyone should try."

John F. Kennedy

Lauren Williamson was getting dressed for high school while she casually watched the morning news on TV. It was the morning of September 11, 2001, and as she dressed, she saw a plane crash into a New York tower. At fifteen, she wasn't sure what the Twin Towers were, but she knew something huge had happened and ran upstairs to wake her mom and dad.

Her mother gasped in pain when she saw the TV screen and realized that her sister might be on that flight. It had never occurred to Lauren that her darling Aunt Betty could be a flight attendant on that plane. But she knew she worked for American Airlines, based in Boston, and Flight 11 was out of that airport. Her father drove her to school, but she was only there for a while before it was evacuated. Her call wouldn't go through to her dad, so she went home with friends. A few hours later, her mom called and began to cry on the phone. Her youngest sister, Betty, had been on the plane that crashed, and all passengers had died on impact. For Lauren, it felt like a light had been extinguished.

Lauren, who looked on Betty as one of her moms, felt the impact in numerous ways. While people in New York who witnessed the attack rallied around each other, Lauren felt isolated in San Francisco. The people she knew were stunned but didn't feel personally connected to the event. Her high school sent a big sympathy card honoring Betty, but at home, her family was overwhelmed with grief, and her little brother, Austin, was asking Lauren for help with his sadness.

Telling the initial story

Lauren remembers that the hardest aspect of that day was witnessing her mom having to tell her grandparents that their youngest child, Betty, or Bee, as they called her, had been killed. Lauren's grandparents sat in their living room, frozen. Her grandmother was strong and digested the news, but her grandfather couldn't believe it. He kept saying, "She'll call soon. She's all right."

Over the days, the family learned that Aunty Betty had been one of the distinguished heroes on the day of 9/11. While the terrorist attack was taking place on Flight 11 from Boston, she stood in the back of the plane, not knowing if they would kill her, and made a twenty-three-minute call to flight personnel on the ground. Her call, the first alert to anyone about the hijackings, is now part of recorded history, and her extreme bravery has been highlighted. Lauren later spoke to the woman who received Betty's call. She reported how calm Betty was, as she gave vital information that caused the FAA to close US airspace for the first time in history.

Hearing about her aunt's heroics

The family flew to New York and visited the rubble of Ground Zero while it was still smoldering. This was the first of many trips that they would take over the years. Even when she doesn't make a pilgrimage to the site, Lauren still listens for her aunt's name in the annual reading out of people lost on that day. However, Lauren doesn't see her aunt's death as a tragedy. In the big picture, she witnessed how much impact one person can have when they show strength and dedication to serving others. This realization was a turning point for Lauren that continues to inspire her today.

Over the years, her family united in finding meaningful ways to honor Aunt Bee. They collaborated with a pastor to rename a recreation center in Chinatown to be called the Betty Ong Recreation Center, and years later, when President Obama came there to honor her aunt and give a speech on immigration, Lauren was chosen to sing the Star-Spangled Banner. Her family also created the non-profit Betty Ong Foundation to provide summer camps for underserved children and the elderly. In 2018, a memorial honoring Betty Ong was held at the Hyatt in Burlingame, and over one hundred flight attendants flew in to attend it.

Helping other mothers

The strength of Lauren's matrilineal family tree: her grandmother, still living today at ninety-nine, her mother, and her aunt Betty, has infused Lauren's life with inspiration and purpose. Through her high-achieving career, Lauren met and married Justin, and a few years later, they started trying to have a baby. It turned into an arduous IVF process that took many attempts over several years. In a desire to help others, Lauren posted on Instagram, offering to help other women going through the same challenging process. Since there is no guarantee of success, people often get discouraged and don't know where to turn. Hundreds of women turned to Lauren online for counsel, and she advised them, "There's no guarantee that you will have a baby, but in the big picture, it is certain that you will learn from the process, and you will transform."

While posting about IVF, Lauren started telling stories about her Aunt Betty. She told people that because of her aunt Betty's nickname, Bee, Lauren had always had a positive association with bees. When she got pregnant with her daughter, Olivia, people joyfully sent her gifts, a stuffed bee for her baby and a baby blanket with a bee motif.

Inheriting Aunt Betty's Story

Olivia, who is almost three and too young to know the story of Aunt Betty, stuns Lauren and the rest of the family by spontaneously mentioning Aunt Betty. When Olivia first saw pictures of horses — one of Betty's passions in life —she pointed and said, "Auntie Betty." Lauren's grandmother, the honored hub of the family, notices little ways that the joyful, carefree Olivia reminds her of Betty as a child, and she and Olivia love spending time together.

Lauren often feels Aunt Betty's presence and openly shares her view: "I think Aunt Betty is part of us, not apart from us. She is part of me and of Olivia and of all of us, and I see evidence of that every day. Our family has so much joy, I can't believe how blessed we are, and in March, after more IVF challenges, we are going to have a little boy."

This story of Aunt Betty will take on more meaning for Olivia as she gets older and can understand how bravely her great-aunt tried to save people all over the country. Olivia will grow up with the understanding that courage runs in her family.

Reflective questions:

Has there ever been a tragedy that focused your family on a common purpose? How has your family handled loss?

Resources:

Noel, Brook, and Blair Pamela, PhD, *I Wasn't Ready to Say Goodbye, Surviving, Coping, and Healing after the Sudden Death of a Loved One*, Sourcebooks, 2008.

Best Thing: Draw Strength from Your Ancestors

"I have great respect for the past, if you don't know where you come from, you don't know where you're going."

Maya Angelou

When Jodie Patterson wanted to draw strength during a time of challenge, she liked to drive south to her ancestral family home, and she loved to look at the photos of her African- American ancestors. The South renewed her. It was the place where she could always rediscover who she was as a woman and a mother. Being in her family home always put her challenges in perspective. Her grandmother, Gloria, had earned a Ph.D., had several divorces, and had been arrested twenty-five times for protesting. Her aunt Lurma had also been arrested for protesting thirteen times before she was twelve years old. Jodie's current issues as a parent weren't related to race, but they did require an ability to act courageously and put her life in perspective. When Jodie's third child, Penelope, was three, she announced that she was a boy and insisted she be treated as one. This event propelled Jodie into endless questions about how to raise a trans child.

Over the last several years, Jodie had completely exhausted herself trying to make the world a more accepting place for Penelope. As a mother, Jodie saw herself as the person who should be able to create a supportive community for her daughter. But Jodie needed a break and decided to leave Penelope and her other three children at home and travel south with her oldest daughter, Georgia, who would be leaving for college soon. The trip would be a chance for them to connect and for Georgia to learn more about their matrilineal line. Jodie's grandmother, Gloria, isn't alive anymore, but her mother lives in her grandmother's house, and Jodie finds it peaceful to be with her mom surrounded by so many memories. Jodie sometimes resents her mother's lack of initiative in facing challenges head-on. However, nearing her mother's house, Jodie could feel her mind slowing down as she drove through the winding Southern streets.

Hearing her husband's perspective

For several years, Jodie had been partnering with her husband Joe in deciding how to understand Penelope's daily wants and needs. But, like so many moms, she felt like the only one who could carry the responsibility for her child's well-being. Jodie read widely about the experiences of trans people and, per Penelope's requests, asked family members to address her with male pronouns and to give her boy gifts for her birthday and Christmas. Because Jodie was working to understand these issues so fully, she sometimes felt frustrated that her husband failed to adopt the same perspectives.

When Jodie proposed the idea of going to a trans family camp, Joe agreed. As soon as they arrived, Joe was delighted to see one of his college friends, which immediately made him more comfortable. Jodie was heartened when Joe openly expressed his feelings during discussions in a group for dad, and it helped her understand his thinking. They simply had different perceptions of their children, and she noted that other fathers had similar points of view. They seemed to like approaching change more slowly. The camp allowed both to share intimate feelings, which could be validated by others. Jodie had lots of anxiety and "What if" questions about Penelope and how people would treat her as she got older. She felt guilty for not knowing how to make changes in the world so children like Penelope would feel supported.

After arriving at her mother's house, Jodie engaged in her usual revitalizing activity of looking at photos of her matrilineal ancestors and thinking about their lives. They had been leaders in their families, and thought of themselves as strong women, not to be knocked over by the problems of the world around them.

Restoring after taking so much responsibility

Being at her mother's house also helped Jodie release her mind from a problem-solving mode and experience a feeling of ease in life. Sitting at the table in her mother's kitchen with her daughter, Georgia, who was suddenly so grown-up, Jodie suddenly realized that she and Georgia are the inheritors of that matrilineal line of strong women, and as such, they both possess wisdom.

A few minutes later, Georgia demonstrated her wise perspective by asking Jodie curiously, "Why don't you just see Penelope as normal?" Jodie immediately understood the underlying meaning in her daughter's query, and it caused an epiphany. She realized Georgia was asking, "Why don't you look at the big picture and see that you're not the only one responsible for Penelope's development?" Jodie realized that in Georgia's generation, it was common for people to adopt gender identities that express their inner beings rather than their birth gender. That was one of the ways the world was changing, and her adolescent daughter, Georgia, didn't see her younger sister, Penelope, as a problem to be solved.

Jodie also recognized that it was tapping into the courage of their legacy that had allowed this mother/daughter conversation to happen.

Stepping into collaboration and shared care

Jodie's book, *Big Bold Family*, shares her journey and her capacity for looking at the big picture to discover and rediscover her true identity in an ever-changing world. Like her ancestors, Jodie has been able to rally with like-minded people and collaborate on a shared goal. Her memoir reveals all the people who supported Penelope: family members, the teachers at her wonderful private school, friends, and an outstanding karate coach who led Penelope to an amazing karate victory. In her book, Jodie provides a role model for looking at the big ancestral picture of our legacy and believing in our own abilities to create a new narrative.

Reflective Questions:

Are there family members who inspired you by the way they handled a challenge?

Is there any departed relative whose voice helps you in hard times?

Resources:

Nealy, Elijah, PhD, *Transgender Kids and Teens: Pride, Joy, and Families in Transition.* W.W. Norton and Company, 2017.

Patterson, Jodie, *A Bold World: A Memoir of Family and Transformation,* Ballantine, 2019.

Best Thing: Make Family Disagreements Okay

"It is grief that develops the powers of the mind."

Marcel Proust

Coleen loved her family's Catholic faith growing up and attended Catholic schools from kindergarten through college. As a child, she felt close to her parish priest and talked to him about personal problems, and he encouraged her soul searching. Her parents were strict Catholics, but Coleen's interest in spirituality broadened as she got older.

She married in her early thirties, and she and her husband, Seth, had a baby right away, and they named her Ashley. A couple of years later, she got pregnant with a second child, another little girl, and they were both thrilled. However, a genetic test showed that the fetus had problems and that her daughter would probably never be able to breathe without a ventilator. Seth's immediate choice was to terminate the pregnancy, even though Coleen's parents would be upset.

However, Coleen wasn't ready to make that decision, and she meditated on the big picture and what life would be like for her second daughter. Would she be happy to be born with the simple gift of life? Or would never being able to breathe on her own feel like a terrible burden? She tried to teleport into her unborn baby's heart and mind and have a sense of her future. Finally, Coleen came to the conclusion that relieving the baby of a painful, constricting life was the best thing to do. Although she felt tremendous grief at not giving birth and having a life with this little girl, she went ahead with the termination.

A few months later, she had a second pregnancy with the exact same outcome, a girl who wouldn't be able to breathe on her own, and Coleen and her husband again decided to terminate.

Focusing on her grief

Both decisions were terribly hard and invited censure from her friends and, of course, her parents. One woman's reaction was, "I could never do that!" Her mother was very upset, critical, and embarrassed about Coleen's choice, and this added to the grief that Coleen was already feeling. It was hard for her mother or anyone else to understand that Coleen felt a connection to the souls of the little girls. Around this time, Coleen discovered a book called *Spirit Babies* by Walter Mackitchen, a book for prospective parents trying to attract the soul or essence of a particular baby residing in the spirit world into their family.

This wasn't exactly Coleen's situation, but it led her to contact a psychic, a woman who lived in her community, whom she asked about the little girls she had lost. The psychic reassured her that her daughters were doing all right, leaving Coleen with the feeling she had made the right decision. She also went back to her parish priest, who expressed great compassion toward her. These were the things she intuited she had to do in order to move on.

It was on Christmas Eve a couple of years later when a beautiful Christmas parade made its way down her street, with people dressed as angels and singing lovely carols. They stopped at her house, and her whole family came outside. The event felt like a blessing, and that night she conceived another baby, a little boy whom they named Peter. He grew into a vigorous child, a fun little brother for Ashley. However, Coleen has never forgotten her connection with the little girls that she lost.

Learning to dialogue

This isn't a subject she feels comfortable talking about with her mom, or most people. Coleen understands and empathizes with those who are pro-life since she advocates for life in all its forms. She believes that these can be divisive issues, partly because it's almost impossible to put her delicate feelings about her decision into words. Coleen had gone to the deepest part of her knowing and empathy for the children she was carrying. It wasn't a decision made lightly or out of inconvenience or expense for a medically fragile child. Most importantly, the process helped her discover that her intuitive senses really mattered in the long run.

The journey gave her a different perspective on being a mother and a daughter to her own mom. In addition, she was affected by a podcast she listened to with psychotherapist and author, Dr. Harriet Lerner, discussing women's relationships with their mothers. The interviewer presented the phenomenon that so many daughters are so challenged in relating to their mothers that they cut off contact. Lerner responded compassionately to these difficulties and said in her practice, she urges women to adopt an attitude of curiosity toward their mothers. Her recommendation actually reflects construal theory. Adopting a curious mindset takes us out of the ruminating mind and helps us to time-travel back into our psychological/spiritual heritage.

One of Lerner's recommendations is to develop the strength to disagree with one's mother rather than cutting off all contact. She suggests that being able to say, "I feel differently about that subject," is an important achievement in the mother/child relationship. It allows the daughter to establish herself as an individual with boundaries while still being able to have conversations—a benefit to both parties.

Teaching her children to feel comfortable with differences

Coleen has taken this to heart, not only with her mother, but with her two children. When they are discussing a subject where they don't easily agree, she will purposely say, "Maybe, we have different ideas about this, and that's okay." Coleen is a very sensitive listener with her children and encourages them to fully express their feelings and ideas, even when they are counter to hers.

Reflective questions:

How do you handle differing perspectives with family and friends?

What do you teach your children about having views different than yours?

Resources:

Lerner, Harriet, PhD, *The Dance of Connection,* Harper, 2009

Makichen, Walter, *Spirit Babies: How to Communicate with the Child You're Meant to Have,* Delta, 2005

Best Thing: Appreciate Those Who Support You through Change

*"Acceptance, tolerance, bravery, compassion, these
are the things my mother taught me."*

Lady Gaga

Throughout her many changes and busy public life, Glennon Doyle has appreciated her mom's steadfast support and has eulogized her in print while her mom is still alive. Glennon credits her mother for teaching her that in the big picture, what really matters is love and "relentlessly showing up for people." Her message to her mom: "Never did I feel alone. You showed up again and again. That is what family is. That is love. That is your legacy."

Glennon has built and rebuilt her sense of self. She overcame struggles with bulimia and addiction when she became a mom in 2008. She also started a blog called *Momastery* to share her life experiences as a progressive Christian and mother. Even as a religious writer, Glennon's prose has always been prized for its authenticity; she referred in print to her pregnancy test with her first child as "an eviction notice," kicking her out of her wild lifestyle. She remembers thinking, "What if this is an invitation to shed my identity as a drunk and bulimic and start another role: mother?" Over the next few years, she became the mother of three children with her husband, Greg Melton. In 2016, Glennon wrote a book that integrated her unflinching honesty about herself and her faith, called *Love Warrior.* As an Oprah-recommended book, it became an instant bestseller.

She continually offers her wisdom about the process of her constant metamorphoses and tells women: *"You are not the sandcastle, you are not the builder, I am not at the end of the day, a mother, a wife, a writer, an activist. I am a child of God, and I can build again and again."*

Ability to be there through change

When her husband Greg revealed he had been unfaithful to her throughout their marriage, Doyle entered another metamorphosis and started searching again for her real self. This is the kind of lifequake Bruce Feiler suggests happens several times in a lifetime. Her mother accepted each of her changing identities, including falling in love with another woman, Amy Wamback, and marrying her in 2017. Glennon's relationship with Amy and her new perspective on life propelled her to become a gay activist. In 2020, she wrote *Untamed*, which sold more than a million copies. In 2021, she and Amy launched a podcast called *We Can Do Hard Things.* They continue to co-parent their three children and with the children's dad, Greg, and hold regular family dinners. Her mom has been the hub of the dynamic family all along.

Role models for showing up

Glennon was profoundly moved to witness her mother's relationship and devotion to her own mother when she was dying. She writes, "And then there was this past year, Mama. This year, your best friend, your mama, died. And you took her hand, even though you were both shaking, and you walked her home. You moved back to Ohio, and you, your brothers, and sisters spent months sleeping on the floor beside her bed, waking five times a night to shift her and give her medicine."

What Glennon sees in her mother is the capacity for loving actions, not just words. Glennon's mother has never told her daughter how she should be but has always accepted each person she has become. Glennon wants her children to grow up having the same sense she did as a child, that there was never a moment when she wasn't adored. She believes that adoration between mother and daughter is the gift of her matrilineal family tree.

Reflective questions:

What allows a mother to accept and support a child's shifts in identity?

Resources:

Doyle, Glennon, "To My Mama, Who Taught Me the Most Important Thing," *Momastery*. March 2015.

Doyle, Glennon, *Love Warrior,* Flatiron Books, September 2016.

Doyle, Glennon, *Untamed,* Dial Press, March 2020.

Chapter Three: The Big Picture of Reimagining Pregnancy, Birth, and Infancy

"Birth is not just for making babies. It's about making mothers strong, competent, capable, who trust themselves and believe in their inner strength."

Barbara Katz Rothman

Years ago, when my children were young, I traveled as a journalist to interview a well-known female politician, whom I had never met but admired. I wanted to hear her plans for the future, and I was happy to have a contract to write an article about her. I had lots of questions prepared for the interview; I was interested in her background and how she had gotten involved in politics. We chatted amicably, and I loved hearing about her vision for the country. However, that was a very small part of our conversation. What did we end up talking about? The story of her labor and delivery with her baby girl, who was now about eight months old.

I was fascinated and awed by her birth story and her passion for telling it. Labor and delivery are transformative events in the lives of women, and there are few venues for them to share their birth experiences. She and her husband had been excited to be the first in their extended families to decide to have a home birth. As is so often the case, the birth didn't go exactly as planned, but the woman was refreshingly honest about the dramatic details. In an intense moment, her resourceful husband couldn't find scissors and ended up biting through the umbilical cord. The birth was successful, and I got to feel like I had gone through the exhilarating experience with her.

Later, I included the details of her labor and delivery in my magazine article along with my admiration for this famous woman who willingly shared details about a subject that most people keep private. Throughout history, mothers have always been a nurturing audience for each other. In an upcoming chapter, we will explore the patriarchal gag rule about women's health issues and the importance of women talking openly about their experiences.

If the subject of having a baby arises in a group of mothers, women are often eager to retell their stories, no matter how long ago the events occurred. The listener knows that in the mother's mind, the story of her pregnancy and birth remains vivid. Traditionally, birth stories used to be told around the hearth or the kitchen table. Today, they are often told online, but wherever women tell them, they hold the same power. There is the implicit awe for the miracle of bringing a baby into the world, but going through labor and delivery is an arduous process, and sometimes, the stories contain trauma and long-held grief. Whatever the outcome, telling a birth story often rekindles vulnerability and sometimes feelings of loss or guilt. Birth stories and the ability to tell them are often the key to mental health, especially postpartum, as it was for the woman I interviewed. Telling birth stories has also been a way of educating other women.

What is your role in your birth story?

In my work with parents, the most important aspects of birth stories have always been how women characterize themselves before, during, and after the birth. Are they compassionate with themselves over events that didn't play out the way they had hoped? Can they look at the big picture and applaud their own bravery and resilience? Are they able to confide fearful thoughts to a trusted person? Can they mourn the loss of a baby through miscarriage or stillbirth in a meaningful way? For me, the mother is the central figure, needing self-compassion and confidence to nurture a loving relationship with her child.

In this chapter, I have focused on the transition to motherhood as it occurs through pregnancy, birth, and infancy.

But now I would like to stop and imagine how pregnancy and birth might look for mothers, fathers, and babies in an ideal world. What's the most substantive way to support women through "matrescence," the physical, emotional, hormonal, and social aspects of becoming a mother? These questions have become part of our national consciousness. The burgeoning fields of maternal well-being, mental health, and perinatal psychiatry have come into being because people have imagined what women and families need and put those ideas into action. Prioritizing maternal health also reflects an acknowledgement that there are systemic problems in our health care system that disproportionately affect marginalized groups. The United States has one of the highest rates of maternal mortality among wealthy countries, and Black women are three times more likely to die from pregnancy and related complications than white women. In 2021, legislators introduced the Black Maternal Momnibus to address these health disparities, and in 2023, Congress established a Federal Task Force on Maternal Mental Health. Then, on Mothers' Day 2022, the Health and Human Services Department launched a National Maternal Health Hotline for pregnant or postpartum women to call professional counselors at any hour of the day or night.

There are also private programs like Prospera, a mental health support service founded by psychologist, Andrea Niles which trains mothers to be counselors for other mothers in need. There has also been a renaissance in the use of midwives and doulas to support women through pregnancy, birth and early mothering driven by imaginings of a more personalized, holistic vision of what women need.

If you have given birth, no matter how long ago, your story may involve many other people who helped you during various stages of the transition to motherhood. Writing out the details is a way for you to frame your narrative to promote feelings of agency and self-worth as well as to create family legacy and community. Sharing your story can help your children understand their own origins and think about how they want to approach parenthood in the future. Your birth story should be an affirmation of your bravery and resilience. You might even write a love letter to yourself that recognizes both your resilience and vulnerability and showers your former self with any additional support you wish you had. What might that additional nurturing look like?

Where do birth stories lead?

As a keeper of women's stories, I am interested in where birth stories lead and their effect on the relationship between the woman and her child. This isn't the focus of the countless books that typically inform us about pregnancy and birth. In fact, a woman today can probably access more facts on the subject in an hour online than her grandmother had available to her in her whole life. With information, however, comes more complexity and more choice. I have witnessed that the way a woman frames her pregnancy and birth can shape her outlook on herself and the way she views mothering. Does she see in the big picture that it is her connection with herself and her child that matters? Does she see herself as having agency and the ability to advocate for herself and for her child?

In my first book, *The Inner Parent*, written with Marti Keller, we explored how the fantasies mothers and fathers had when they contemplated having a child related to their experience of their everyday parenthood. That's why the trajectory of the birth stories at the end of this chapter doesn't conclude with the first time a mother holds her newborn. Instead, they follow the mother's path of growth, sometimes over a few months and occasionally years. They include the vital support of fathers, relatives, and friends. Since I have had the privilege of thinking with women about the big picture of their lives. I am convinced that sharing the way pregnancy, birth, and early mothering influenced their parenting benefits everyone.

In today's social media world, online stories often fuel competition between mothers by pushing images of perfection, while unvarnished birth stories often contain the tales of shattered fantasies, plans undone, and gratitude for seen and unseen sources of support. Prioritizing authenticity and self-compassion helps us focus on what truly matters to us. Then, we can create our own narrative about pregnancy and delivery without guilt and self-judgment and celebrate our ability to plan with love and make tough choices, even when they differ from our plans or others' opinions.

How does the big picture highlight our values?

The decisions made during pregnancy and birth aren't always based on logic. Often, people's intuitive knowing runs counter to what seems rational. Some of women's most wonderful, life-changing experiences are the result of extreme challenges and even loss. When things are easy and go according to plan, our understanding isn't forced to stretch and expand, but whatever the situation, it's the ability to remember again and again what's important to us in the long run that has lasting value.

Here are some practical suggestions to consider before childbirth:

- Imagine all the ways that nature has prepared your body in miraculous ways to nurture you through pregnancy and birth.

- Build a support network of people you would like to know and love your child once they are born.

- Educate yourself and invite your partner or childbirth coach to learn about childbirth, common birth scenarios, potential interventions, and the options open to you.

- Visualize a positive, self-affirming birth experience.

- Practice positive affirmations like "I am strong and I am worthy of a positive birth experience".

- Express fears, concerns, and preferences with your partner and health care provider and collaborate about realistic expectations.

- Avoid catastrophizing and practice ways of talking about birth in realistic ways with your partner.

- Learn pain management skills and practice with a partner or birth coach.

- Develop a birth plan that prioritizes your well-being, self-worth, and safety over rigid ideas and doctrines.

- Talk about your birth plan ahead of time with your partner and/or those who will be present at the birth.

- Avoid ideas of success and failure when it comes to giving birth.

- Share concerns with others who listen to you with empathy and curiosity, rather than judgment.

- Connect with other expecting parents in classes or online.

- Journal about fantasies, mixed feelings, anxieties, and joyful experiences you are looking forward to with your child in future years.

- Develop a care plan for after the birth that includes ways of managing stress and getting rest.

In this chapter, I have again chosen stories of real women who have experienced challenges and received support in different ways. They all demonstrated strength and resourcefulness that surprised even them and led to important new learning.

Reflective questions:

How were values about pregnancy, childbirth, and infant care passed down in your family?

Resources:

Carlsson, Marie. "The Relationship between Childbirth Self-efficacy and Aspects of Well-being, Birth Interventions, and Outcomes,". PubMed, October 2015.

Fieres, Jamie, "Birth Your Story: Why Writing Birth Stories Matters," Santosha Birth and Wellness, September 2017.

Goidel, Coleen, "So You're Pregnant! What Are You Telling Yourself about Birth?" Blog post, June 16, 2020 (Co-founder Two Doulas and You.)

Isaacs, Susan, Keller Marti, *The Inner Parent,* Harcourt, Brace, Jovanovich, 1978,

Jones, Lucy, *Matrescence, On Pregnancy, Childbirth, and Motherhood,* Pantheon, 2024.

Tolman, Allison, *Birth Affirmation Coloring Book*, Vervante, 2019.

Here are the stories:

In the first story, Sarah is surprised by pregnancy at forty. She pours all her excitement into making idyllic plans for a natural birth and successful breastfeeding. Her strength, however, turns out to be the ability to pivot as she meets obstacles and finally experiences a turning point as a new mother when her pediatrician helps her to see the big picture.

In the second story, Corinna talks to her baby in the womb like a trusted friend and makes promises to him about how wonderful their life together will be. However, as a mom, there are lifequakes and disruptions to that plan. Later, she loves finding ways to make good on all those commitments.

In the third story, Annie experiences horrific fantasies about her newborn. It takes courage for her to confide them to her husband, but doing so starts a journey of amazing communication between them that lasts to this day.

In the fourth story, Hannah has to make a heart-rending decision about whether to risk her life to save her unborn daughter. Witnessing her own bravery allows her to change her life and her career.

In the fifth story, though far from her Australian roots, Rani decides to have a home birth. Her ability to make that decision and immerse herself emotionally and spiritually in the process was inspired by the book *Gentle Birth, Gentle Mothering* by Dr. Sarah Bentley.

Best Thing: Be Ready to Pivot from Your Plans

"Life is tough, my darling, but so are you." –

Stephanie Bennett Henry

How do mothers maintain self-worth and redefine being a good mother when their ideal plans for pregnancy, birth, and motherhood are disrupted?

When Sarah discovered she was pregnant with a baby girl at the age of forty, she and her partner, Russ were thrilled and decided right away to name her Izzy. Sarah's best friend since grade school is a birth doula, and through the years of talking with her and other mothers, Sarah became extremely knowledgeable about childbirth. As a result, she started early in the pregnancy to focus her mind on positive thoughts that would avert worry and wrote inspiring affirmations about labor and delivery:

"Nature does not hurry, yet all is accomplished."
"Relax, soften, open; My breath is helping me stay
calm and centered.:

These affirmations helped her feel calm and confident about facing birth with a steady mind. Sarah wanted to have her baby at home, but she was advised not to because of her age. She decided to use a birthing center, but it was an hour away, and the center was already at capacity. Sarah finally realized that she would have to go to a traditional hospital to give birth. After readjusting to that idea, she put all her love for the new baby into her birth plan. She wrote it out and went over it many times with her midwife, doula, and her mom.

Sarah engaged in voluminous research about natural birth and decided she didn't want to have any drugs in her system, so her baby wouldn't be groggy when she was born. However, more disruptions started occurring in her plan, and Sarah bravely marshaled all her positive thinking into whatever might come next.

Programming a beautiful birth

The day she went into labor, a hurricane was imminent, and there was danger that the roads would be flooded. However, at midnight, she and Russ managed to drive to the hospital after a long day of contractions. Sarah was exhausted but always prepared; she packed scotch tape in her bag, and the first thing she did was to tape all her affirmations on the wall of her hospital room. She also hung a sign saying, *"Happy Birthday Izzy* "to welcome her new daughter.

Flowing with changes

Sarah was planning a water birth, and her midwife helped her into the tub, but by that time, she was tired and in so much pain she finally decided to ask for an epidural. Her midwife kindly supported all her choices. She had to get out of the tub and onto the bed to get an epidural, but by the time she was on the bed, it was too late to administer the epidural, and she had to push. The doctor offered Fentanyl for the pain, and her midwife assured her that if she felt she needed it, it would be short-acting. A few minutes later, her daughter, Izzy was born, and she and Russ focused completely on the wonder of being with her. The plan had changed again and again, but she and her partner had adapted and focused on staying positive and the joy of their daughter, Izzy.

Planning for perfect nursing

Sarah had her heart set on nursing, but again, life threw her several curveballs, and this time it made it hard for her to keep feeling positive about herself. Izzy had tongue, lip, and check ties and had to have laser surgeries. After the surgery, Sarah had to perform painful exercises rubbing Izzy's gums every four hours, and the pain made it difficult for Izzy to latch onto the breast. At the time Sarah was actually triple feeding; breastfeeding, pumping, and bottle feeding, in addition to providing skin to skin contact. On top of all that, she was juggling Izzy's dental follow-ups, her own medical appointments, lactation consultations, studying for her Real Estate exam, and Russ was having spinal surgery. There was never a moment to rest. Sarah found the whole thing heartbreaking. Her perspective was that good mothering and nursing were synonymous, but Izzy wasn't gaining weight and that was worrying. Nevertheless, the lactation consultant advised Amy to start pumping every hour, and she did. She remembers,

Constant nursing and taking care of everything while Russ recovered made life feel completely chaotic and unmanageable. On Facebook, none of the moms expressed empathy with the idea that Sarah should stop nursing no matter how exhausted and overwhelmed she was. Instead, out of good intentions, they tried to help by offering endless hacks to help her continue no matter what. Their reactions increased Sarah's belief that she was a failure for being so tired that she wanted to stop. Her inner dialogue was relentlessly self-shaming, and it was affecting her mental health.

Finally, her pediatrician listened compassionately and told her that, in the big picture, it wouldn't matter in Izzy's life whether Sarah continued nursing or switched to the bottle. He said what mattered was taking care of her own needs and focusing on being with Izzy. He advised her to stop nursing and emphasized that what would count was their loving relationship.

Sarah remembers that whole period poignantly,

A little over a year later, mother and daughter are still involved in their delightful dance of love. Most importantly, Sarah believes in herself as a mother who can stay strong in difficult times, look to the big picture, and pivot when needed.

Reflective questions:

How important do you feel flexibility is in childbirth and new parenting?

Resources:

Chidi, Erica, *Nurturing: A Modern Guide to Pregnancy, Birth, Early Motherhood and Trusting Yourself and Your Body,* Chronicle Books, 2017.

Best Thing: Talk to Your Baby before Birth

"By the third trimester of pregnancy, the auditory system of the baby is well developed. Babies have a preference for the birthing parent's voice because it is so familiar to them."

Dr. Kimberley Bentley

Corinna had longed to have a baby, and she and her husband, Richard, were both thrilled when she became pregnant. She started talking to her son, James, while he was still in utero. She would walk miles every day, talking and talking to him. She would also listen. Corinna confides that she was as interested in James' thoughts as she would be with any intimate friend. They found other ways to communicate. She would give James a loving caress through her stomach, and he would kick back. She felt so happy being pregnant that she felt like she could go on that way forever. However, when his due date passed, Corinna knew he would have to be born soon. Still, she went on for another two weeks, with no contractions and no sign that James was going to emerge from his cozy home.

Promises to her baby

Two weeks after her due date, Corinna drove her husband, Richard, to work at 4 a.m. On the drive home, she had a serious conversation with James. She even made him important promises: "James, I know it's very nice in there, which you and I both love, but I need to tell you that we'll be even closer when you come out. There will be soft blankets, and I'll be able to hold you. There'll be kittens, puppies, and rain. I can't wait to show you rain and puddles. You're going to love it."

This was a significant moment. The promises Corinna made seemed light-hearted and fun, but she viewed them as long-term commitments to James and to herself. She began forming a big picture of all the wonders they would experience together, and over the years, she has worked hard to make that vision a reality.

After talking to James that night about all the delights life would hold, Corinna went into labor. The contractions went on for two days, but she didn't dilate at all. The doctor gave her pain pills. Finally, they had her come into the hospital so they could monitor her labor. A whole crowd, her mother, her husband, her father, her brother, and her brother's children came to the birth so they could greet James the moment he came into the world. Labor progressed, but in the last phase, Corinna couldn't push him out. She pushed for five hours, and he didn't budge. It turned out, James's head was too large, and the doctors were having a hard time helping it pass through her pelvis.

Prayers for a safe delivery

Corinna was scared, and again she focused her attention on talking lovingly to James, "We're in trouble, Buddy. We are really going to have to pray to get you out safely." She agreed to the doctor using suction. James had been in distress and came out crying. However, the minute Corinna said, "Hi!" he listened to her voice and calmed.

After they came home, Corinna's time with James felt idyllic. She and her husband traded off care. She worked at night as a florist, so she had to be with James during the day while Richard worked. She took James everywhere, carrying him in a pack on her chest and talking to him about everything they were doing.

Thoughts about what really matters

Over the years, Corinna felt her marriage had unraveled. When she finally told Richard she wanted to leave the marriage, he protested, saying, "If we divorce, James will have a broken home." This struck a chord with Corinna, and she meditated on the word "broken." In the big picture, she wondered, what would having a broken home mean? She had the disturbing image that James's life would be split in two, with half his time with her and half with his dad. That didn't feel good.

Corinna realized she didn't want that for James. She had told him his life would be full of delight.

- Corinna had a new career and decided to find a home as close as possible to her ex-husband so James could see his father every day if he wanted. That's the way their lives have gone on happily over the years. James is fourteen now and leads a unified life with two homes, along with Corinna's big extended family.

Emotional skill building

Corinna and her sister, Megan, have created the lives they always wanted with their children, and they've done it in concert with their mom. Corinna says, "We mother in a trifecta. We orb around my mother, whom we all call Nana. My sister and I have made all the promises to our children happen, the kitties, the puppies, the huge yard for them to play in, and puddles to jump in. I have dancing in my life, and Megan teaches aikido. We support each other in the most wonderful ways."

The secure bond that she and James formed when he was a baby has lasted and been the foundation for seeing them through many challenges. They still have important conversations daily, and Corinna helps him navigate emotional challenges in his life.

The vows Corinna made to James when he was inside her body were commitments she made to herself and she is grateful that she has been able to fulfill them.

Reflective questions:

Does a relationship form between mother and baby before birth?

Is there communication?

Resources:

Baron-Cohen, Kate Lindley, PhD, "Mom's Baby Talk Boosts Infant Oxytocin," Neuroscience News, Report on a study at the University of London College, Department of Psychology, London, 2024.

Hazan, Cindy, and Campa, Mary, *Human Bonding: The Science of Affectional Ties,* Guilford Press, 2013.

Best Thing: Trust Someone with Your Fears

"Having intrusive postpartum thoughts can leave you feeling ashamed, afraid, and stressed, especially scary unwanted thoughts often come on suddenly without warning. Some thoughts and images may occur once, while others may repeat or occur constantly."

UPMC Health

Annie was married in May and discovered she was pregnant in July, right after starting her medical residency. She was surprised by the pregnancy but immediately rallied and found a great birth class that she and her husband, Tom, could take. Several of the lessons focused on pain management. That's when Annie and Tom started learning how to become real partners in communication to establish a foundation for working together as parents. They practiced mental distancing during contractions by exploring a fantasy that would diffuse pain. Annie told Tom she wanted to take a mental trip to the beach during labor. And many times, Tom patiently talked her through the details of relaxing on the sand.

Taking a workshop on communication

The class inspired them to do more work on developing communication tools as a couple. They were newlyweds and knew the first year was supposed to be hard, but neither of them had good role models for empathetic communication between adults in their childhoods. Annie's parents had a contentious divorce, and her father's new wife was very critical of Annie. Tom's parents didn't divorce, but they didn't really communicate. So, Annie and Tom signed up for an online class in couples' communication with the Gottman Institute. It turned out to be one of the best decisions they made.

They found these classes were empowering and gave them great tools for future communication as parents, as well as during labor and delivery. As it happened, Annie ended up having a Caesarian. After all her preparation for a natural birth, she was disappointed, but she and Tom were happy to bring their baby, Kayla, home; however, in some ways, having a new baby to care for ushered in a terrifying chapter of their life.

The terrifying spiral of scary thoughts

Annie was a loving, conscientious mom, but her pre-birth anxiety didn't go away, and she was tired from her residency. She started having frightening thoughts at night when she was putting Kayla to sleep. Sometimes, she would look at how fragile Kayla was and suddenly think, "What if I hurt her? What if I put a pillow over her and smothered her?"

Annie was shocked by these thoughts. Where did they come from? But the scary images persisted, and they were so disturbing that Annie began to characterize herself as a bad person and a danger to her child. She was afraid she had become a monster. Her spiraling thoughts prevented her from having access to the big picture of how loving and attentive her care was with Kayla. She never disclosed her self-immolating thoughts to anyone, and she sometimes felt suicidal.

After months of her self-criticism in terrifying control, Annie finally confided these terrible thoughts to Tom, who was very empathic. He reassured her that everybody has negative thoughts, but that didn't mean they would act on them. He urged her to get help. Finally, Annie made an excruciatingly difficult decision to see a doctor. Her regular OB was out of town, so she had to see another doctor. However, their conversation left her feeling worse. The doctor told her the only way to get rid of her dark thoughts was to pray. Annie felt irate and knew she needed to find someone more knowledgeable.

The power of mental health support

Annie found a therapist who specialized in cognitive behavioral therapy and post-partum depression. The therapist told Annie she could see she was a very caring, protective mom who would never hurt Kayla. The therapist taught Annie to mentally distance herself from her negative thoughts and try not to give them any weight. She told Annie to imagine thoughts coming and going like clouds in the sky. This was similar to the zooming out techniques she and Tom had learned for pain management during her birth class. Annie was relieved and began to read the books on intrusive thoughts and postpartum depression that the therapist suggested.

It was life-changing for Annie to realize that in the big picture she had been a devoted mother and not the monster she had imagined herself to be. She likened her inner world to the scene in Moana when the heroine faces the lava monster, Te Ka with empathy, returns her stolen heart, and transforms her back into the goddess Te Fiti. In retrospect, Annie came to see that she had been a newlywed going the extra mile to learn communication tools as well as a medical intern who carried on meticulous tasks every day, in spite of torrents of her own self-abusive talk.

This realization was a huge turning point. She could see that life was really the opposite of what her negative thoughts had been telling her. This was a powerful lesson. However, she was still acutely aware of how hard her depression during pregnancy had been a couple of years later when she and Tom started talking about having another baby.

A second pregnancy

Annie and Tom explored the idea of how a second pregnancy might go. They talked about what would happen if Annie became depressed again and had to endure the onslaught of frightening thoughts. Remembering how close they had grown through that difficult time, Tom expressed faith in Annie and their ability to handle challenges together, and Annie, who had worked so hard to recognize the signs of depression, expressed her conviction that she could act proactively.

Annie did get pregnant, but it was a different experience because she wasn't in her residency and wasn't tired all the time. However, in the fourth month, she had a huge reaction to a small event and realized she was starting to get depressed from the hormones. Her therapist put her on an antidepressant that wouldn't harm the baby. She also had perspective about her pregnancy. Annie hadn't known anything about intrusive thoughts in her first pregnancy or the symptoms of depression, but now she knew how to let things go. Whenever a negative thought came up, she discarded it without giving it weight. After her second baby, Mollie, was born, Annie was happy and okay during the whole postpartum period, and their family bubbled with delightful activity.

Through therapy, she also learned that she had an enormous ability for honest self-reflection. She had learned to pay attention to her self-talk during high-stress situations. Annie is still grateful for all the hard work she and Tom had put into their communication. It will be the foundation of co-parenting in happy, mutually supportive ways for years to come. She reports that they try hard to parent their daughters in a way that reflects their values, giving each daughter the support she needs.

Reflective questions:

How does shame play a role in keeping women from getting the help they need?

Resources:

Kleiman, Karen, Wenzel, Amy, Waller, Hilary, Mandel, Amy Adler, *Dropping the Baby and Other Scary Thoughts: Breaking the Cycle of Unwanted Thoughts in Parenthood*, Taylor and Francis, 2017.

Gottman, John, MD, and Silver, Nan, The *Seven Principles of Making Marriage Work*, Harmony Books, 2015.

Best Thing: Create the Perfect Environment for Birth

"When you see a woman who isn't frightened, who is giving birth without interference, you stand back in awe."

Ina May Gaskin.

Deciding to have a home birth was a first in Rani's large family. She grew up in Australia, and her mother had eight children, all born in the hospital. As the fifth child, Rani was close to her two brothers, Jack and Bill. Rani married an American and moved to Pennsylvania, where her husband Kevin's family lives, but she still communicates frequently with her close family down under. When Rani told her brothers that she wanted her baby to be born at home, they decided to come from Australia with their mom to be with her during the birth. Rani was happy to have her family with her. She found taking walks with her brothers soothing while she was having early contractions for several days. Everyone admired Rani's level of preparation with her midwives and her calm conviction about how birth would go. Since she wasn't having medical interventions at her home birth, Rani was determined to be completely in control of keeping her environment the way she envisioned.

Preparation for gentle motherhood

Rani had studied early childhood education in college and formed an interest in high nurture communities, which involve parents placing emphasis on being responsive to babies and young children. Rani and Kevin felt that having a natural home birth would build the foundation for the kind of connected, gentle parenting they wanted for their baby.

Rani especially loved the book, *Gentle Birth, Gentle Mothering, A Doctor's Guide to Natural Childbirth, and Gentle Early Parenting Choices* by Dr. Sarah Buckley, and it became her guide. Dr. Buckley used her own birth stories and parenting to illustrate what she calls "undisturbed birth" or "physiologic birth." Over thousands of years, Dr. Buckley describes the hormonal process as evolving to help women give birth. The book describes the woman's body as containing a "hormonal blueprint," the perfect blend of hormones and strength to provide an "ecstatic birth experience." Buckley emphasizes that this process only occurs if it isn't "disturbed" through distractions in the environment.

Rani knew that taking advantage of birth hormones during a natural birth would require all her focused concentration. As a result, she told her family ahead of time that she would need to create a state of quiet and harmonious balance even with all their activities. Rani worked with her midwives in advance to make a plan for the day of the birth.

Gentle birth approach to contractions

When active labor began, she found it hard to concentrate on the contractions with everyone around, so she asked her family to go back to the apartment where they were staying. That left Rani, Kevin, the midwives, Mayumi, Carol, and Devin. and her dear friend, Pat, together when labor intensified.

As part of her training for the Buckley method, Rani had learned about animal birth experiences. As a result, she kept the image of animals needing to go into isolation to give birth as her labor progressed. "My understanding of it is to create an environment in which the pregnant woman is free to birth without distraction, as much as possible." She noted that mammals are quiet when they are going to birth and usually seclude themselves to allow the natural physiological process to proceed with ease. Indeed, being able to establish quiet gave her a surge of confidence in her ability to relax into the contracting waves sweeping through her body.

Entering a transcendental state

The silence helped her to enter what she describes as a "transcendental state" and surrender to the contractions which were then coming with little break. It was painful, and they went on for eight hours. Suddenly, she realized she was in transition with the strong urge to push. For the first time, it felt like the baby passing through her might split her in half. Then, there was the push and rush of baby Rohan coming into the world right there in their living room surrounded by the loving, completely peaceful presence of her husband and her incredible support team. At the moment of birthing, she cried out to Meher Baba and her father who had passed away the previous year. She also suddenly felt extreme gratitude for her mom, who had given birth to eight children.

The home birth fulfilled Rani and Kevin's vision of an ideal way to bring Rohan into the world, which empowered her immediately to engage in the responsive parenting practices she had read about. One of the methods was called "elimination communication." It involves tuning into the baby's cues, so they can eliminate bodily waste into a little potty. Rani and Kevin found it easy to pay close attention to Rohan and put her on the tiny portable potty.

Elimination communication is considered a way of developing a strong bond with a baby and to help mothers more fully understand a baby's cries. It is widely used in Asia. Since babies don't wear diapers, elimination communication prevents diaper rash and helps the environment because disposable diapers produce enormous waste in production and disposal.

At five months, Rohan is thriving, and Rani feels fulfilled. She plans to stay home with her for the first three years, the developmental time when she views high nurturance to be crucial. Her husband has been off during this period but plans to return to work.

Thinking about the many ways that birth takes place and the setbacks women experience, Rani feels blessed to have been able to follow her birth plan. Although there were no disruptions, her ability to feel emotionally and physically in sync with her baby was based on the decisions she made about her own needs for quiet.

 In the big picture, she saw herself and her baby, Rohan, united in an intricate dance, both making a huge transition simultaneously. Rohan was transitioning into family life and Rani into gentle motherhood. Rani has written out her birth story in loving detail, and someday she will be able to share it with Rohan and recapture the feeling of those loving first moments when they became a family.

Reflective questions:

What is the role of teamwork in allowing women agency in childbirth?

Resources:

Buckley, Sarah, MD, *Gentle Birth, Gentle Mothering; A Doctor's Guide to Natural Childbirth and Gentle Early Parenting Choices,* Celestial Books, 2008.

Olson, Andrea, *Go Diaper Free: A Simple Handbook for Elimination Communication,* The Tiny World Company, May 2015.

Chapter Four: The Big Picture of Collaborating to Create Well-being

"It is my earnest wish that women can commonly come to prioritize, and to regularly receive themselves, the steadfast love and care that is uniquely associated with mothering."

Suniya Luthar

How do we know children?

I still humorously refer to my dear friend, Mimi, as the "good mother" in our family, and my children, though grown, still cherish her wisdom in their lives. My first book was accepted by a publisher the day after my third baby, Mari was born, and I learned they would be sending my co-author and me on a book tour. My husband couldn't go or stay home with the children, so I needed help. I couldn't afford to pay a nanny, but a friend told us about Mimi, a young writer who needed a place to live, and we offered her a free bedroom in trade for part-time help with the baby. Mimi and I took all three kids on the tour and became close friends.

Later, when I was a single parent, Mimi moved in with me again, and when I was overwhelmed by pressures at work and felt guilty about my long hours, I reassured myself with positive self-talk like, "They have Mimi stepping in as their good mother." Telling myself that they could get nurturing from many sources allowed me to see the big picture of parenting and relieved me of worry and stress. Mimi also helped me know each of my children as individuals, and when one of them was having a problem, I could always turn to her for fresh insights. Since she wasn't their biological parent, she didn't see them through a lens of worry or self-blame but as separate people with unique characteristics and life journeys.

Mimi is what Professor Sarah Hrdy calls an "allo" or supplementary mother, and Hrdy makes a case that throughout history, allomothers have been extremely important. This term comes from the Greek word "allo," meaning "other," and in recent years, the words "allomother" have crept into common parlance, referring to someone who collaborates with a mother to nurture and care for her children through cooperative childrearing. There is even an app to locate allomothers.

In her book, *Mothers and Others: The Evolutionary Origins of Mutual Understanding,* Sarah Hrdy introduces the historical significance of females, in animal species as well as human, helping biological mothers. There is even a hypothesis that grandmothers evolved to play this special role. Hrdy also describes current hunter/gatherer cultures and the specific ways allomothers support the biological mother so she can do her work for the group as well as care for her children. Hrdy and other anthropologists point to the evolutionary importance of allomothers in the development of socially adaptive, empathic human beings who have received love from many sources. Hrdy's view is that women have always "worked" and needed additional help from relatives and community members to sustain their energy for many tasks, as well as to aid in their children's development.

Thinking back, I would have to contrast my own experience of having Mimi's help after my third baby with my first post-partum period eight years earlier. When my first baby was born, we moved to an area near my husband's job where I didn't know anyone. I was in love with my newborn son, as I was with all my babies; in fact, I turned down a part-time teaching job at the local university to stay home with him. However, this was an unexpectedly hard adjustment because I felt so isolated. It was wonderful getting to see every aspect of my son's development, but I missed adult company, especially during the day. I would see other mothers chatting in the park, but I didn't know how to connect with them. So, I found another way to get the support I needed. At least once a week, I would hop on the bus with my son in his carrier to travel twenty-five miles to my parents' house. Fortunately, both of them had passionately embraced grandparenting, and when I arrived, I felt buoyed by their enjoyment of my son and the ability to share all the new things he was doing. Interestingly, Sarah Hrdy writes that throughout history, grandparents, especially maternal grandmothers, have been super-star alloparents.

Of course, my other huge support was my husband, who was fully engaged the minute he stepped in the door after work. In anthropological literature, fathers are also referred to as alloparents.

Their participation in child-rearing is viewed as supplemental because there is substantial variability in male involvement with the young across different animal species and human cultures. But historically, most dependable alloparentng has come from other females.

After some time, I managed to find an alloparent when my son was still a toddler. I created a food co-op for our urban neighborhood, buying healthy food in bulk and distributing it to other families. The woman who started it with me had children the same age, so it worked well for us to become alloparents for one another, and in addition, our project helped our family and other parents economically. I was tremendously grateful that this mutual support continued after my second baby, Gabrielle was born.

How can we make child-rearing supportive?

If you are a mother, dear reader, I want you to be able to find others to support you, reduce your worry, and help you understand the children who come into your life. As Hrdy advises, when you are thinking about having a child, start thinking ahead about collaboration. Ask yourself whether you will have a partner and who your allomothers might be. Whether you are planning on staying home or going back to work, unquestionably, allomothers can help achieve balance and well-being in your life if you can find them. When it comes to parenting, we all need collaboration.

As someone who has worked closely with parents over decades, I have witnessed that child-rearing needs to be a collaborative process. That's what it was in the past. The modern idea that mothers should be all-knowing repositories of knowledge and the ones to blame if anything goes wrong in a child's life is an unfortunate, cultural narrative that undermines women and weakens our society.

When most people lived in close-knit communities, it was understood that it takes a village" to raise a child was not just a metaphor. People were vitally interested in children and invested in making them good community members. Family and neighbors offered suggestions about their development. In a holistic sense, the community's concerns about children served to safeguard them. In contrast, the mid-20th-century portrayal of a mother as the only one responsible for her child's development has created an impossible expectation of perfection: the image of a mom who should know everything about her children and effortlessly manage their lives. The well-being of the mother, the role of the father, the child's inborn traits, and the influences of other people are usually left out of the picture.

How did the father of attachment theory receive nurturing?

English psychoanalyst, Donald Winnicott, considered one of the founders of the maternal/infant attachment theory, is famous for his concept of the "good enough mother," someone attuned to a child's development, though not always perfectly. Winnicott also provides an example of the importance of other people in a child's life through the story of his own childhood. As an adult he reported that his mother experienced bouts of depression, and as a result, he reported feeling nurtured by "multiple mothers," grandmothers, aunts, and his beloved nannie.

How fortunate for Winnicott's mother that she had allomothers, both relatives and non-relatives, who stepped in to support and fully love her son. The nurturing they offered may have informed Winnicott's concept of the good enough mother. It is often cited today as evidence that we need to decrease the pressure on mothers and view their roles more compassionately. His forgiving vision allows us to think from the perspective of a bigger picture.

In the complexity of modern life and changing family structures, it is vital for us to embrace a paradigm that supports mothers and recognizes the importance of other people's roles in the lives of our children. We need to create communities of caring that encourage adults to understand and nurture each other's children. To explore the concept of caring communities, let's start with our own childhoods and analyze the ways we were nurtured.

Who loved you into being?

Fred Rogers, the renowned creator of the long-running TV show, *Mr. Rogers' Neighborhood*, offered viewers a profound but simple method for understanding the reality that even when we have challenging relationships growing up, on some level, we all exist in a force field of love.

In 1997, after receiving an Emmy, Mr. Rogers asked the viewing audience to stop and think about their own childhoods. "We all have special people who love us into being. Can we take ten seconds to think about those people and thank them?"

Dear reader, indulge me as well by pausing for a moment to think about those who "loved you into being." Were there people in your childhood who really saw and understood you as a unique person? Were there other adults who gave you mothering besides your mom? Were there animals, a dog, a cat, or a horse that nurtured you? Cast a broad net to picture the people or creatures who couldn't wait to know you even before you were born. See if you can reabsorb some of the caring they felt for you.

In the previous chapter, we heard women's birth stories, and they all reveal collaboration in action. Those narratives highlight the important role that husbands, midwives, doulas, mothers, brothers, aunts, uncles, and grandmothers play in supporting women through the huge transition to motherhood. In fact, parents need caring communities not just after becoming a parent, but throughout childrearing. They need trusted figures in their lives to help them navigate a rapidly changing world where familial roles are being reshaped and people are expected to communicate in unprecedented ways.

How are families changing?

We only have to look around to see that the nuclear family with a father, mother, and their biological offspring is no longer the norm. Sociocultural changes and technological advances have allowed us to redefine the family in flexible ways. Men have become more involved in childcare, extended families have made a resurgence, parents are embedded in social networks, and more children are raised by unmarried parents who live together, as well as step-parents and same-sex parents. Today, one in five fathers has become the primary caregiver in their homes. What kind of collaborative support do these people need in their caregiving roles?

Furthermore, the number of single women having babies has increased, but that's only part of the story. Statistically, single mothers struggle more than any other group economically and have more challenges finding adequate childcare to enable them to work. On the other hand, single women, women over forty, and married women having problems conceiving are using their financial resources to have babies with the help of IVF. Technology also provides opportunities for gestational surrogacy, a process that allows an individual or a couple to have a woman, often previously unknown to them, to carry and give birth to their child.

Whether mothers are single or married, about 75% work outside the home though the number of hours worked often depends on the age of the children. Today, there are more college-educated women in the workforce than college-educated men. Only ten percent of highly educated mothers elect to stay home, and the choice is so rare that they are called "opt out" mothers.

As a result, alloparents are now more important than they ever have been. As more and more professional women enter the work force, they need to have loving, reliable care for their children, and they increasingly employ nannies to provide it. In the past, nannies were reserved for the very wealthy, and the relationships were hierarchical and with defined duties and relationships. Today, there is an increasingly high demand for nannies among middle-class mothers, and their relationships and the ways a nanny supplements a mother's duties are typically unique to their situation. Some nannies stay in a child's life for years, some for a few months. Many nannies and childcare workers today are mothers themselves and have their own needs for collaborative support. Part of resolving the current childcare crisis is society recognizing the value of women who help other women care for and love their children.

Because our society has overfocused on the attachment between mother and child, we have popularized the negative belief that mothers need to worry about the risk that a child might love the nanny more than them. These concerns serve to make women who work outside the home feel unsure about their own mothering. It also sets up a division between moms who have a choice about staying home and those who work.

We know now that secure attachments are important for psychological well-being, and when they go awry, skilled child therapists can help parents repair those bonds. But we have too narrowly defined children's abilities to love and be nurtured by other adults. We have also left out the fact that new mothers throughout history have learned about their children from listening to the allomother's perspectives. Unquestionably, childcare workers are an extremely important source of collaboration and learning for parents, and there is no doubt that it is important for children to have positive attachments to them.

How do people relate to family members they don't know?

In the changing nature of the modern family, many more women enter into their mothering roles as stepparents. In the past, women typically became stepmothers by marrying a widower whereas today stepparenting more often happens through divorce and remarriage. It's estimated that forty percent of new marriages involve at least one child from another marriage. These newly configured families almost always involve a father continuing to co-parent with his ex-wife while the newly married mother struggles to understand her role in parenting children she may not know well. New stepmothers can feel like outsiders in an already established system and need support and self-compassion to maintain their feelings of worth.

As a new stepmother, women can face quandaries about how to relate to the children's mom. At the same time, the biological mother may worry about how to communicate positively with a new person in her child's life. Women in both situations need support in managing expectations and developing relationships, but we can learn through the authentic stories of women who have become alloparents for one another.

With the rise in families with two dads and two moms, we obviously need more research to understand what supports parents' needs in these families. Studies reveal that same-sex families today are part of the changing face of fostering and adoption, with their willingness to have children of color placed with them and strong communication with birth families.

Since most adoptions today are open, expectations exist for most adoptive parents, heterosexual or same sex, to work with biological families. Today, biological families may include birth fathers as well as birth mothers, and there is no blueprint for communication between adoptive and birth parents who often start out as strangers. But again, women are showing us through their individual stories how they create new kinds of kinship. Several narratives in this book detail women's caring relationships with people who might have become their adversaries without their creative efforts to collaborate.

How do families with special needs get the support they need?

Today, we no longer automatically institutionalize children who are born with special needs, nor do we accuse mothers of causing autism. The book, *Intelligent Love* by Marga Vicedo. tells the story from the 60s of Clara Park who in spite of the fact that she was accused of causing her daughter's autism, went to extraordinary lengths to find creative ways to help her. Clara later documented her innovative process in a book called, *The Siege: The First Eight Years of an Autistic Child.* Vicedo's book tells the exciting story of how a group of parents collaborated to change public perceptions of the causes of autism in spite of the blame laid on mothers by the psychologists of the day.

Today, we aspire to give the estimated 30 % of families who have children with special needs sensitive, collaborative support, and there is widespread awareness that their lives are often stressful. In families that have children with autism spectrum disorders, research shows that mothers and fathers often become skilled collaborators in helping their children in difficult situations, though mothers may spend more time involved in their direct care. Whatever the division of roles or whether a parent has a partner, these families need to feel included in the mainstream so they can trust that their children will be valued and respected. In these cases, as in others, we are fortunately learning through the collaborative communities parents are forming, often online.

What is the role of social media in providing support and/or confusion?

It would be hard to overstate how important online collaboration resources are in the lives of mothers and fathers today, whether they have a typically developing child or one with special needs. There are online forums tailored to the needs of working moms, stay-at-home moms, gay moms, Black moms, Hispanic/Latina moms, and moms who have a child with an illness or have a disability themselves. The number of virtual spaces to hang out with parents who have similar needs and values increases daily. Mothers are typically the ones creating these networks that support parents around the globe. This online outreach can welcome parents from different cultural and income groups into a huge, understanding embrace.

At the same time, looking for answers and connection online is more apt to be a source of confusion and depression for mothers than fathers. The pressures on mothers to create the mythical perfect child can keep them hyper-focused on the ever-changing kaleidoscope of perspectives on parenting. Unhappily, mothers of young children may lose faith in their own intuitive instincts while they are bombarded with other people's perspectives.

The push for mothers to constantly acquire "new knowledge" and to be on the lookout for problems creates an unconscious burden for many women who lack supportive community. Instead of feeling self-compassionate for the oversized expectations society places on them, mothers today often feel guilty that they don't easily have the answers to their children's challenges, which can be a recipe for worry.

In addition, some online mom groups foster toxic competition, criticism, and outright shaming. Controversies about subjects like what mothers feed their children or how to help babies sleep through the night can cloud women's judgment and trigger spirals of negative self-talk. However, women often find that the antidote to those perfection driven controversies comes from relationships with other women who are open to exploring other people's viewpoints.

Why is collaboration between women so historically powerful?

Throughout history, women have shared parenting concerns and responsibilities with other women, Research shows that when women actively support each other, they can experience the experience the same affiliative hormones present in their bodies and brains as they do while bonding with their babies.

In her breakthrough book, The *Tending Instinct: Why Nurturing is Essential to Who We Are and How We Live,* renowned psychologist Dr. Shelley Taylor describes the evolutionary superpower women have possessed through the ages that allows them to support one another in unique ways during crises. In times of extreme stress,

Taylor says women have the ability to transcend their own fight/flight responses and replace fear with the capacity to "tend and befriend." It's hypothesized that this naturally supportive response during a crisis is hard-wired and includes gathering and caring for children and others who are weak.

I would add that an important aspect of women's abilities to tend to each other is their capacity to care for children who are not biologically their own. Even on a day-to-day basis, women step up to help each other recognize when they are doing too much, getting too tired, or not paying attention to their own physical or mental health. Women are aware of the societal pressure for mothers to be all things to all people, and fortunately, the aid they offer can encourage a mother to pay more attention to her own needs.

Who should mothers choose as confidantes?

However, in a competitive culture, there can be another side to communication in friendships between mothers, just as there is online. Mothers can be accusative, critical, and undermining when they feel they must compete to ensure that their children are successful. Interestingly, physiological studies show that the presence of competition between parents reduces" feel-good" hormones in their brains.

Self-compassion guru, Dr. Kristin Neff, says, "With self-compassion, you don't have to feel better than others to feel good about yourself." That's what occurs when mothers help other mothers to see the big picture that real success in the lives of children and adults is feeling self-worth.

In the interest of maintaining inner well-being, *Chatter* author Ethan Cross advises people to be very deliberate about choosing a collaborative partner if the goal is to reduce anxiety. Ethan points out that simply venting about problems often mentally amplifies them. This is especially true when the listener is critical or, on the other hand, joins us in our worry. Ethan advises that stepping out of the worrying brain requires a collaborator who will listen to our feelings and help us see a broader picture. How do fathers fare in that department?

Are fathers supported as full collaborators?

As mentioned earlier, overfocusing on mothers has distracted us from the important role fathers play as attachment figures. Research shows that contrary to the stereotypes, men involved in the care of infants develop and experience a similar level of the affiliative hormones that promote attachment as women. Evidence also shows that men's testosterone levels often drop before birth or adoption. These scientific discoveries are an important factor in our collective understanding. As a society, we need to provide policies that encourage men to take parental leave to bond with their new babies. Studies also show that supportive relationships between partners in providing infant care promote a flow of affiliative hormones in the brains of both people.

Secure attachments between babies and their fathers benefit everyone involved, but become extremely important when a mother experiences post-partum depression, high-work stress, grief, addiction, or illness, all factors that can influence an infant or a child's well-being.

However, if women want men to have close relationships with babies and to participate equally in their care, they must become aware of the natural tendencies that causes them to operate as "gatekeepers" that keep men from physically caring for infants. If women are critical of the ways men relate to babies, they may be discouraging the flow of affiliative hormones that promote attachment. Research shows that men sometimes experience perinatal depression, and one of the causes can be feeling like an outlier in the bonding process. Those early interactions set the stage for future relating and are important in children's social development.

How can women be aware of their own burnout?

In recent decades, discussions about collaboration between men and women have often revolved around whether they have an equal distribution of chores. There is another aspect of childrearing that places an unequal burden on women. Although men are becoming more involved in childcare and domestic tasks, women are usually the default parent in the eyes of the world, the one who takes on the mental load of keeping track of everything in a child's life. This becomes particularly intense when children have medical, psychological, or learning issues and mothers become the project managers for coordinating all their appointments. For society to change, we all have to have a hand in rewriting mothers' job descriptions and re-allocating women's responsibilities.

It's important for working mothers and for couples to recognize the signs of burn-out, a pervasive problem in a culture where women feel they have to perform perfectly at work and at home. It's characterized by chronic stress, physical and emotional fatigue, sleep disturbances, and an overall sense of being overwhelmed. Recognizing the signs of burn-out is crucial for initiating a recovery process, and consequently it's important for couples to talk about how to lessen a mother's load. In order to do that, she has to look at the big picture and recognize all the plates she has in the air and how much she has invested in keeping them spinning.

Pivotal research by Suniya Luthar and Lucia Ciccola shows that the key factors in a mother's well-being are feeling unconditionally loved and comforted when she is in distress. Luthar said, "Just as unconditional acceptance is critical for children, so it is critical for mothers. Mothers, like children, benefit greatly when they know they have reliable sources of comfort in distress from a partner. Women also need a plan for reducing burn-out, becoming a "good enough" mother and worker, and finding activities that nourish them.

The importance of self-care is even more important for moms who are single or divorced. Parents who are divorced can still collaborate effectively and that often depends on having communication tools that allow them to problem-solve with each other in non-critical ways. Today, courts are more balanced about giving fathers joint custody and setting up workable agreements for parents to function successfully together. Whenever parents are trying to collaborate with someone who holds different opinions, the way forward is finding points of convergence. It's also important for them to pay attention to their self-talk and ask themselves what they are telling themselves about their parenting.

Why is collaboration with oneself so important?

Our future as mothers depends on our ability to let go of worn-out stereotypes of what a good mother is and what comprises a healthy family. We can start by paying attention to our inner dialogue on any given day. Do we credit ourselves for all that we do, or do we tell ourselves we aren't doing enough? As mothers, we also need to release ourselves from self-defeating traps of competition. We also need to help recognize signs of depression, extreme stress, and burnout in each other. Furthermore, we must not forget that part of the big picture is fully supporting fathers in their important roles.

 Our age could well be a turning point to create a new paradigm of compassionate collaboration in our communities.

Here are some suggestions for collaborating with other women:

- Look for allo mothers, relatives, friends, nannies, who can provide a loving presence in your child's life.
- Notice and praise other mothers' parenting and self-care.
- Be aware of your own tiredness and burnout and take steps to lessen your mental load and aspirations for perfection.
- Talk about your mental load and feelings of being overwhelmed with your partner and with the alloparents in your life.
- Create inclusive networks and support groups.
- Be aware of your own competitiveness with other mothers as stemming from societal images of "the good mother" and "bad mother."
- Empathize with a mom whose child is having a tantrum and offer to help.
- Avoid judging and gossiping about other mothers' parenting practices online or in person.
- Be transparent with childcare professionals and specialists to give your child support.

Here are some suggestions for co-parenting between mothers and fathers or between same-sex couples:

- Make plans for sharing care before birth.
- Involve partners in baby care from the beginning to promote attachment.
- Talk about feelings of depression or overwhelming stress.

- Take a strength-based approach with each other. Notice what's going right in your partner's relationship with your child, even if you're not together as a couple.
- Avoid gatekeeping and feeling that you know the right way.
- Talk in terms of "I-messages" and stating your needs.
- Point out the way your partner or other parents are following their values even in frustrating situations.
- Reassure your partner and others that there is no such thing as perfection in parenting and encourage them to notice progress.
- Remind each other of how you've gotten through challenges together.
- Study communication as in the Gottman online education for couples.

The mothers in the stories that follow often felt like they faced impossible challenges but learning to collaborate was the foundation for growth.

Reflective questions:

How can we value collaboration more in our society and learn ways to promote understanding?

Can we broaden our understanding of mothering and recognize and nurture the idea of allo-mothering?

Resources

Abraham, Eyal, PhD, Feldman, Ruth, PhD, "The Neurobiology of Human Allomaternal Care; Implications for Fathering, Coparenting, and Children's Social development, "Physiology and Behavior, 2018.

Bentley, Gillian, PhD, Mace Ruth, PhD, editors. *Substitute Parents: Biological and Social Perspectives on Alloparenting in Human Societies*, Berghahn Books, September 2009.

Campbell, Anne, *A Mind of Her Own: The Evolutionary Psychology of Women,* Oxford University Press, 2013.

Diamond, Rachel, PhD, "Do Hormones Impact How We Care for Babies?" Psychology Today, July 2023.

Gottman Institute, *Navigating Different Parenting Styles in Blended Families*, 2024.

Eyal, Maytal, PhD, "Enough with the Mom Guilt Already," Atlantic Magazine, Aug 6, 2025.

Doucleff, Michaeleen, *Hunt, Gather, Parent: What Ancient Cultures Can Teach Us about the Lost Art of Raising Happy, Helpful Little Humans,* Avid Reader Press/ Simon and Shuster, 2021.

Gamson, Joshua, *Modern Families: Stories of Extraordinary Journeys to Kinship,* NYU Press, 2017.

Golumbok, Susan, *Modern Families,* Cambridge, 2015.

Harlow, Teresa, *Combative to Collaborative; The Co-Parenting Code,* Promethean, September 2021,

Hrdy, Sarah Blaffer, *Mothers and Others, The Evolutionary Origins of Mutual Understanding,* Belknap Press, 2011.

Kahr, Brett, *D.W. Winnicott: A Biographical Portrait,* Routledge, May 2018.

Kristjanson, Karen, *Co-parenting from the Inside Out: Voices of Moms and Dads*, Dundurn Press, 2017.

Landers, Susan, MD. "Your Journey through Working Mother Burnout- From Recovery to Resilience." Posted February 2024.

Livingston, Gretchen," *Opting Out? About 10 % of Highly Educated Moms Are Staying at Home,",* Pew Research Center, May 2014.

Luthar, Suniya, *PhD, Ciciolla, Lucia, PhD,* "Who's Mommy? Factors that Contribute to Mothers' Well-being," a study published in an online edition of Developmental Psychology, 2015.

McDonald, Cameron Lynne, *Shadow Mothers: Nannies, Au Pairs and the Micropolitics of Mothering,* University of California Press, 2011.

Salam, Maya, "College-Educated Women Are the Workplace Majority, But Still Don't Get Their Share," In Her Words, July 2, 2019.

Salas-Betsch, Isabela," The Economic Status of Single Mothers" CAP, August 2024.

Schaeffer, Katherine, Aragao, Carolina," Key Facts about Moms in the U.S. ", Pew Research Center, May 2023.

Sear, Rebecca," Beyond the Nuclear family: an Evolutionary Perspective on Parenting," Current Opinion in Psychology, Volume 7, February 2016, Pages 98-103.

Schaeffer, Katherine, Aragao, Carolina," Key Facts about Moms in the U.S." Pew Research Center.

May 2023

Spencer-, Wood, PhD, Suzanne, Seifer, Laura, MA, *Mothering and Archeology: Past and Present Perspectives, Routledge*, 2025.

Strauss, Elissa, *When You Care: The Unexpected Magic of Caring for Others,* Gallery Books, 2024

Taylor, Shelley, *The Tending Instinct: Women, Why Nurturing is Essential to Who We are And How We Live, Macmillan*, 2002.

Walton, Alice, PhD, "6 Ways Social Media Affects Our Mental Health,*"* Forbes Magazine, June 2017.

Yardie Baby.com, "The Working Mother's Guide to Collaboration: How to Succeed by Working Together," Blog post, Nov 28, 2023.

Here are the stories:

In the first story, we meet Abby and Amy, two women who have wonderful husbands but process the challenges in their teens' lives through their friendship and the alloparentng of each other's children. They show us what it really looks like for women to unconditionally support each other.

In the second story, we hear the surprising tale of Darla who decided to become a foster mom when she was 60. She never could have imagined all the people she would meet and collaborate with as a result. But her whole family stepped up to the challenge and reinvented itself to include and love the biological family of their new son.

In the third story, Melanie and Aaron find resources and ways of collaborating that help their adolescent daughter through an unexpected, but dire psychological crisis.

In the fourth story, we go biblical with Alicia Jo Rabins, a Jewish scholar, who had to turn to the example of Moses to justify asking her husband for more help even though he was stretched. Fortunately, the couple was aided by a therapist to work out the common challenges that modern, overwhelmed couples often face.

In the fifth story we see the value of authenticity in helping mothers maintain their self-worth. Fanny felt that the specialists assessing her son's speech were not seeing the same child she witnessed playing and talking at home. She wasn't intimidated by having to make hard decisions and during the process, she opened herself to seeing her son in new ways.

In the sixth story, we see the miraculous potential for collaboration to support children in a blended family. Bianca was wary of her partner's ex as she eased into the role of stepmother, and at first, she judged her. However, as she saw the quality that came from the biological mom's bond with her stepdaughter, she realized that they could be alloparents for each other,

I hope these stories inspire you to write your own story of collaboration as a parent.

Best Thing: Gain Perspective from Alloparents

e.e. Cummings

Both Abby and Amy are mothers of teenagers and business partners. They have super-supportive husbands, but when it comes to figuring out what's going on with their kids, or with their own emotional lives, they consistently turn to each other. From the time their children were young, that's the way the two friends have grounded themselves and moved forward- in mutually supportive ways. They have been consistent allomothers for one another for years. Abby says, "Amy knows me better than anyone, and if I start to get into one of my panics as a mother, she'll say, "You're doing that thing you do again. "That's when I realize I'm worrying, and it's not helpful. She's always there to convince me everything is going to be all right in the big picture."

"We are truth tellers to each other," Amy says. "We know each other's patterns. When there is a challenge at work, I often get angry, and Abby encourages me to go on a walk. Abby's pattern is to react to stress with fear or panic. I've learned to try to help her reframe situations, so she doesn't get as anxious."

The power of women helping women

Research shows that mothers often get their most vital support from other women. In part, it's because women tend to pay more attention to emotions and ask questions before making a decision. Amy and Abby have had a lot of choices and situations to navigate in their business and in their lives as mothers.

Now, after eight years, the business is on solid footing, but the two women are still having continual discussions about the best ways to support their children as they launch into the world. They feel that their collaboration results in wisdom – a bigger picture of what really matters to them.

A woman-run business

Eight years ago, the two women looked at the big picture of their lives working as teachers and decided to risk everything for their dream. They left their jobs to start a unique drop-in art program for children and families called I Heart Art, offering curated art experiences to children of every age.

Amy and Abby each have two children, but they collaborate on mothering all four kids, who are now adolescents and young adults. The children frequently helped at the art program when the two women were creating the business, and in this way, the families came to love and understand each other. The two women have collaborated in meaningful ways to address many challenges.

Big child-rearing challenges

Over these years, they have explored ways to help each of their children through major transitions. The women also have strong parenting collaborations with their husbands, but their friendship adds another dimension to understand their children. The women have appreciated their ability to discuss issues deeply with each other. In a way, the relationships between the two families provide the same knowing as an extended family.

Their mutual challenges have included supporting:

- A socially awkward high-school boy, picking a college where he flourished and found a love interest with a young woman.

- An academically gifted adolescent daughter, coming out as gay and looking for a high-end academic college with a diverse student body.

- A teenage daughter, navigating a steady relationship with her boyfriend, raising questions about sexuality, and entering the world of parties and alcohol safely.

- A physically strong teenage daughter, finding her central meaning in life through hiking and camping adventures, asking to travel around the world alone.

All of these challenges require soul searching and an ability for each of these mothers to look at the big picture to alleviate anxiety about their kids. Amy and Abby's friendship is a living testimony to the fact that collaborating can pull us out of ruminating and allow us to take constructive action. Again and again, these two friends have listened to each other and enhanced their abilities to listen deeply to each of their children. Since they know each other's children so well, each can provide a wider lens on a problem to the other. In effect, they act psychologically like surrogate mothers who help each other zoom out of worry to think in a big picture way about challenges that arise.

"We want our kids to know they can come to us because we view mistakes as part of growing up and because we will support them." Abby says, "However, it's not always easy to know how to support them day to day in the best way possible. But with our mutual knowledge of these children, we can foster a belief in our children's abilities to make good choices, in spite of occasional mistakes."

While Abby and Amy deeply appreciate their wonderful husbands, it is their daily conversations that reassure them and help them stay positive, as their children move into a very complicated world. Their friendship illustrates the pivotal role women play when they collaborate and see the children as unique individuals.

Reflective questions:

How can parents learn to care about other people's children and form more caring communities?

How can we establish the importance of allomothers in a woman's life?

Resources:

Goleman, Daniel, PhD, and Boyatzis, Richard, PhD, *Social Intelligence and the Biology of Leadership* by Harvard Business Review, 2008.

Best Thing: Create New Forms of Family

*"Call it a clan, call it a network, call it a tribe, call
it a family: whatever you call it, whoever you are,
you need one."*

Jane Howard

Darla was over 60 when she surprised her family by saying she wanted to take in a foster child. With her daughter away at college, she found that her job wasn't bringing meaning into her life. It was 2017, and Darla wanted to do something to create a better world. Darla, her husband Steven, and her daughter, Joelle, all agreed that the love of a foster child would add to their lives even though they had no clear concept of what that would be like.

Welcoming a new family member

As a result, Darla and her husband applied as foster parents and several months later welcomed a handsome two-year-old named Eugenio into their home. Darla was thrilled to show him his new room, his toys, and especially looked forward to signing him up at the private school her daughter, Joelle, had attended. Since he had experienced trauma in the past, she was able to get him a free therapist through the county. She and Eugenio met with Lucretia right away, and the relationship proved invaluable in helping her navigate her new role.

Lucretia told Darla that in the big picture, it was crucial for Eugenio to have ongoing relationships with his birth family, or later he would ask himself, "Why didn't they care about me?" Darla hadn't thought about this in any depth before becoming a foster mom, but she understood what Lucretia meant, and she wanted the best for Eugenio. However, making a bridge with his biological family felt challenging.

Bridging with the biological family

A whole string of new people had entered Darla's life. They included Eugenio's biological mom, only two years older than Darla's daughter, Joelle; Eugenio's father, who was in jail; Eugenio's grandmother, Paula, who was only sixteen years younger than Darla;

Paula's two teenage sons; Eugenio's court-appointed attorney; and two social workers. Whew!

Darla began taking Eugenio on supervised visits with his mother. His mom tried to be consistent, but over time, she wasn't able to get to the visits during the appointed time, and ultimately, she stopped coming. Since he no longer had predictable times with his mother, Darla began bringing Eugenio to court-appointed visits with Grandmother Paula, who clearly loved the little boy very much.

Darla had no access to Eugenio's records, but she assumed he must have been homeless at some point because when he first started living with them, he had a ritual of moving things before bed. One time when she tried to change his diaper, he yelled, "Get away from me, bitch." There were other behavioral flare-ups, but eventually life settled into a routine: dropping Eugenio at preschool, going to her full-time job every day, meeting weekly with his therapist, and taking him to visit his grandmother. In the midst of their new life, Darla and Steven were developing a trusting bond with their foster child.

Then, about a year and a half later, Darla heard shocking news: Eugenio's father had been murdered. This was scary for Darla and devastating for his mother, Eugenio's grandmother, Paula. He was her oldest child and losing him caused her enormous grief. Darla felt for her because, as a single parent trying to raise two teenage sons, she already had challenges in her life. Since Eugenio's mother was unable to go forward with a reunification plan, the county held a hearing to terminate her parental rights.

Coming up with a life-changing idea

The legal process initiated a new life-changing idea: Darla and Steven realized they had fallen in love with Eugenio and decided to try to adopt him, even though they were both over 60. What would happen to Eugenio if something happened to them? They hadn't started the journey with the intent of adopting, but during their time together, they had become family. He felt like their son.

They hired an attorney, but that was just the beginning of a complex process. Eugenio's social workers were adamant that he should be adopted by his grandmother, Paula, because she was his biological family. As a result, they were hostile to Darla during the court proceedings, and it took bravery for Darla to hear them testify against her every session, and it went on in that tense way for several months. Finally, Eugenio's court-appointed attorney visited him both at home and school and recommended Darla and Steven's request for adoption, and the court found in their favor.

During their visits, Darla and Paula had developed respect for each other and a harmonious collaboration. Through their love for Eugenio, they became still closer, and now, after six years, they feel like a true family. Darla and Joelle helped Paula's son fill out financial aid forms for college and were thrilled that he is the first person in their family to study beyond high school. "We're family now, that's forever, and we have a plan in place for the future. If something happens to Steven and Darla before Eugenio grows up, his sister Joelle has agreed to care for him. If she enters a long-term relationship, that person will know in advance that her brother Eugenio is part of their family."

Eugenio is still in therapy, and Darla has hired a skilled tutor for him four times a week. Paula is still in touch with Eugenio's biological mom and reports that she is very happy to hear her son is flourishing. Darla's family and Paula's extended family, his teachers, his therapist, and all the people who care for him make up a village. That's what every child needs.

Reflective questions:

How can we dissolve the idea of "the other" in our society and make compassionate relationships the norm?

Resources

Goldberg, Abbie, PhD, *Open-Adoption and Diverse Families: Complex Relationships in a Digital Age,* Oxford University Press, 2019.

Best Thing: Learn to Ask for Help

"Asking for help with shame says: You have power over me. Asking with condescension says: I have the power over you. But asking for help with gratitude says, we have the power to help each other."

Amanda Palmer.

Despite all her accomplishments and wide-ranging interests, Alicia assumed she would stay home with her children and let her husband, Aaron, work the same way her mother did with Alicia's father. She reflects, "I didn't consider the fact that I am passionate about my career or that Aaron and I are both self-employed and our work paid our rent."

Alicia Jo Rabins is a poet, musician, singer, writer, and Jewish scholar with degrees in creative writing, poetry, Jewish gender, and women's studies. She also has a great sense of humor and has written a book called *Even God Had Bad Parenting Days, Ancient Jewish Wisdom for Parents*. Her book connects her personal dilemmas of being a mother to her two children, Sylvia and Elijah with Biblical stories, often with hilarious results.

Trading Places

When Alicia became pregnant and realized that economically they would both have to continue working, they made a simple plan: they would take turns caring for the baby while the other worked. The problem they didn't foresee was that it meant only one of them could work at a time, and competition started to build over who would work the most hours in a given week. One of them would go off with a computer to a coffee shop, while the other was on childcare duty, trying to figure out how many freelance hours they would get in that week. Alicia's conclusion:" This was bad for our marriage."

It took a year of fighting for them to figure out that jockeying back and forth for work time was hurting their relationship. They knew they had to get help with their daughter, but Alicia was resistant to sending Sylvia to daycare. She had to sort out her feelings that hiring daycare didn't mean she was failing as a mom. However, it turned out that finding good daycare totally changed her perspective. She was happier because daycare allowed her to fully engage in work and give Sylvia her full attention when she was with her.

Asking for even more help

The other bigger challenge for Alicia was figuring out how to ask her husband, Aaron, for even more help than he was giving. She felt he was by nature supportive, so she hesitated to ask him for more. However, as a mother, Alicia had different needs for support after having a baby that couldn't be put aside.

She felt shame about demanding help from Aaron every evening, often in a harsh way, and she knew the process was driving them apart. Their positions about why they each couldn't do more had become hardened. At the time, Alicia felt isolated and alone and realized she didn't know how to ask for help in a positive way.

Using Moses as a role model

In the big picture, they both realized their arguing was taking a toll on their marriage. In her book, Alicia writes about how they finally got help through couples' therapy. She is candid that it took a wider lens for her to understand that learning to ask for help was part of being an adult. Furthermore, her big picture widened to be more gigantic than most, reaching all the way back to Moses when he became the official leader of the Israelites, which she likened to her new role as a mom. She points out that Moses staggered under the weight of meeting people's needs from morning until night. Finally, his father-in-law Jethro asked, "Why do you act alone?" Moses explains to Jethro that only he can settle people's disputes, but Jethro disagrees, "It isn't right, you will surely wear yourself out!" Instead, he advises Moses to appoint wise people to lead groups ranging in size from ten to thousands.

From her newfound parent perspective, Alicia says, "I have a hunch that Moses needed to admit his limitations and step back from the fantasy of total control." As a mom, Alicia knew that Jethro's words were crucial for her too. Mothers can't do it alone; they will wear themselves out. They need to collaborate.

Alicia was fortunate to find a daycare provider she trusted and that Sylvia enjoyed. That was an easy fit, and she finally had an alloparent support her and give her new perspectives on her child.

Reflective questions?

How can we promote allomothering in our society, so women don't feel ashamed of asking for the help they need?

Resources:

Kleinman, Karen, MSW, LCSW, *What About Us? A New Parents' Guide to Safeguard Your Over-anxious, Over-extended, Sleep-deprived Relationship,* Familus, 2021.

Rabins, Alicia Jo, *Even God Has Bad Parenting Days,* Berman House Publishers, 2022.

Rosenberger, Marshall, PhD, *Nonviolent Communication, Tools for Healthy Relations:* PuddleDancer Press, 2015

Rodsky, Eve, *The Fair Play Deck, A Couple's Conversation Deck for Prioritizing What's Import*ant, Clarkson Potter Publishers, 2020.

Best Thing: Join Together in Learning during Crisis

"Coming together is a beginning; keeping together is progress; working together is success."

Henry Ford

Before they had children, Melanie and Aaron enjoyed their careers in environmental education and traveled widely. They were thrilled when she became pregnant. They named their new baby, Sasha, and she and Aaron were both highly involved in her care and development. That interest actually inspired Malanie to study child development and subsequently led her into a new career as an early childhood educator, a job that she adored.

Aaron became interested in education too, and after some time, he took a job as a middle school teacher at the school that Sasha had started attending when she was in kindergarten. Aaron experienced a steep learning curve to become an accomplished teacher, but he found that he loved the role that had come to him unexpectedly in midlife. These were exciting changes, and Melanie and Aaron, both supported each other in their exciting career undertakings, but their main focus was always on Sasha. They were a family of learners, and Sasha enjoyed school and became a voracious reader. She also enjoyed the Montessori emphasis on exploration in her elementary school, and her teachers reported that she got along well with her friends.

Witnessing an abrupt change

Then everything changed. Sasha, who had been the ideal student, started having grave difficulties. In seventh grade, she started having scary facial and body tics. Lying on the floor doing homework, her legs would randomly flail out. Her arms would jerk unexpectedly, too, and once she almost stabbed herself with a fork while eating. She fell, and there was constant danger of her falling. There were also symptoms that seemed to relate to her eyesight and brain. Suddenly, she could no longer read words because they appeared to jump off the page, and sometimes she saw colors surrounding them.

Melanie and Aaron were very concerned and took her to a neurologist, but the tests didn't show anything. A visit with a therapist revealed that Sasha was extremely anxious, and some of her comments indicated that she might harm herself. Her friends noticed aberrations in her behavior, and Sasha felt too embarrassed and overwhelmed to go to school, and she dropped out. A very insightful teacher at her school recommended a county-run early intervention treatment center for adolescents who appear to be at risk for developing psychosis. Although Sasha wasn't assessed as being psychotic, she was given medication and accepted into the program. As part of the treatment, Melanie and Aaron became full participants, going to family therapy and support groups with other parents. All of these rapid changes brought their abilities to collaborate as parents to help their beloved child into sharp focus.

Assuming a new, overwhelming role

When Sasha started exhibiting worrisome symptoms, Melanie gave up the teaching job she loved. Being home all day with Sasha and witnessing her struggles triggered Melanie's anxiety. In addition, she became the person carrying the responsibility of doing everything to try to manage her care: arranging Sasha's medical appointments, her tutoring, and coordinating all the communication with the school district. Her concerns over Sasha's condition escalated day by day, and she began to resent Aaron for his continued focus on teaching and his apparent ability to compartmentalize Sasha's issues as a side issue in his life.

Melanie felt isolated and overwhelmed by Sasha's problems and confronted Aaron about his ability to dismiss what his daughter was going through, resulting in everything falling on her shoulders. Aaron listened empathically to Melanie's complaints about becoming the default parent and apologized. He understood that she was in charge of managing everything but didn't know what to do because he couldn't neglect his teaching job since that was their only source of income. They decided to connect more fully by having a ten-minute check-in every morning about what was going on that day. Making that decision also helped Melanie to feel more empowered to express her needs to Aaron.

Becoming dedicated collaborators

Their check-ins had another significant benefit; they ensured that as parents, they stayed on the same page with their daughter, who was now studying remotely through the school district. Sometimes, Sasha didn't want to get out of bed or go online. They both agreed that they couldn't force her to do schoolwork, but they collaborated on finding ways to encourage her to keep up with her coursework and maintain her connection with the therapist and coordinator from the school district. Being in sync with each other was the way they got through each day and week, as they tried to keep Sasha moving forward academically. She also received emotional support and encouragement from her therapy providers in the county program. Then, and after several years of hard work by the whole family, the practitioners felt she was finally ready to graduate from the program. This was a huge step.

Learning to support herself

Melanie also decided to find ways to support herself. Since there is so much stigma connected with mental health issues, she didn't feel safe discussing Sasha's issues with others. In other words, Melanie didn't have an allomother who could listen to her stress and step in to help with Sasha. She and Aaron were in the often-isolated world of the nuclear family with no grandparents or close relatives to help. So, Melanie started journaling. In some ways, journaling took the place of having a confidante who could provide her with the emotional and physical relief she needed day after exhausting day. She got some of that from her loving relationship with Aaron. However, Melanie realized that her self-worth had diminished from staying home focusing on her daughter's issues, and she decided to become her own best friend by documenting all the positive actions she took every day. As a result, her self-talk changed, and she could see that in the big picture, she was helping her daughter in remarkable ways.

Learning about her own mind

Melanie's absorption in Sasha's progress, as well as her daughter's diagnosis of ADHD, spurred her to be interested in the way her own mind worked, even though she was an adult. Through assessments, Melanie learned that both she and her daughter were neurodivergent, though not in exactly the same ways. An important part of Melanie's learning was that girls often learn to mask their symptoms of neurodivergence growing up and aren't as often diagnosed. Melanie understands now that Sasha's ability to mask her internal struggles resulted in the fact that she and Aaron didn't notice subtle developmental differences when she was young. In retrospect, they think the onset of puberty caused the dramatic changes in Sasha's behavior that propelled them to get help.

Celebrating remarkable progress

After graduating from the county program, Sasha surprised her parents by saying she wanted to graduate from high school and attend the ceremony with her classmates. That goal motivated her to work hard and catch up, and she had to apply herself diligently to be able to graduate on time. It was a race to the finish, but her efforts paid off, and Sasha was able to graduate with her class. More recently, she has started taking in-person classes at a community college and is enjoying discovering what her interests and talents are, making new friendships, and thinking about what her future might hold.

Melanie has also gone back to working part-time as an educator, but a big part of her life is still supporting her daughter's experimentation with a fuller academic and social life. She and Aaron are both aware that Sasha's journey still requires them to be fully engaged, and they feel gratitude for all the help they received from the county program for at risk adolescents and for each other as collaborative partners. It often takes huge challenges in life to spur our awareness that parenting is a collaborative venture, and it requires effort for people to become the best team players and supporters they can be.

Reflective questions:

How can society support parents whose children develop mental health challenges?

What can we do to erase the stigma surrounding these issues for people of every age?

References:

Greene, Ross, PhD, *Lost at School: Why Our Kids with Behavioral Challenges Are Falling through the Cracks and How We Can Help Them,* Lives in the Balance, 2015

Best Thing: Be Authentic with Professionals

*"There can be no keener revelation of a society's
soul than the way it treats its children."*

Nelson Mandela

Fanny delighted in her second child, Sean, and describes him as a cuddler. He didn't talk as much as his older brother, William, but he and his brother loved playing together. Fanny took the initiative and signed Sean up for speech therapy when he was only eighteen months, which he continued even after he started preschool. However, the preschool teachers were concerned about his development and suggested that he have further assessment.

Failing to see the whole child

The assessment process proved stressful for both Fanny and Sean. Fanny had to bring Sean to an office in a public school where various specialists took turns prompting him to do tasks. She felt there was no warmth to the interaction, and she wasn't surprised when he didn't respond to them. It was hard for Fanny to watch Sean's discomfort, and she expressed her concern that the assessments wouldn't be accurate because of that. The assessment team was sympathetic to Fanny's sense that it was a difficult situation for Sean. They were kind but continued on with their tasks.

It would have been easy for Fanny to feel intimidated in this situation, but instead, she persevered in trying to get them to see Sean as a whole person. She sent them videos she had taken of him talking and singing at home. The specialists thanked Fanny but said they could not use the videos as part of their evaluation. Fanny felt increasingly stressed but relied on the unconditional love from her husband, George, and her family to preserve her well-being during the testing process.

Finally, the school district called Fanny and George to a meeting for a report on Sean's test scores. Fanny found the process agonizing and spoke up during the meeting about how verbal Sean was at home and how engaged he was playing with his brother. She again referred to the videos she had provided.

At the end of the meeting, the specialists shared their conclusions that the only way that the school district could offer Sean more than a few hours a week of speech therapy was if he entered a daily program designed for children with autism. In response, Fanny was honest about her perceptions, but she remained open and vulnerable, "I don't think Sean has autism. He is a completely different child at home than the one you saw in your office. But I'm not a professional, and we are open to your feedback." The specialists listened but kept a professional distance and reassured Fanny and George that they could take time to make up their minds about whether they wanted to enroll Sean in the autism program.

Making a big picture choice

Fanny and George felt like it was a double bind. Ethically, Fanny could not agree with checking the autism box and labeling her child in this way: "It was like they were making me sign a piece of paper saying that Sean is different. It didn't feel right to me. They had not held up their end of the bargain and done enough testing."

She and George finally decided that in the big picture, Sean getting the support he needed at this critical time in his development was the priority, so they signed him up for the special education preschool, designed in part for children with autism.

Finding her people

Some weeks later, Fanny accompanied Sean to his first special education preschool class. When she saw that Sean was the highest functioning student in the class, she was still concerned that they had made the wrong decision. However, after several days, Fanny fell in love with the special education teacher who took time every day to tell her about all of Sean's successes. Fanny felt that she had found a collaborative partner, someone who saw all of Sean and gave him every ounce of her support.

The teacher also taught Fanny to see Sean in a fuller, more knowledgeable way. The teacher explained how each activity targeted the exact areas Sean needed, and he was moving through them comfortably. Sean continued to make great progress over his two years in the program, and this fall, he is going to be mainstreamed into a typical kindergarten.

Fanny has also grown in fundamental ways that surprised her. She confesses that previously; she saw an important part of mothering as worrying about the future. Were her kids meeting their milestones? Would they be able to attend a good college? Get good jobs? It isn't that she thinks her sons won't be able to do any of those things, but her lens has widened in her big new picture of life. Her priority is for her children to have happy, fulfilling lives, being who they are.

"I have such a deep appreciation for everything about both my sons now. Every achievement is a cause for celebration in their lives. I have the chance now for Sean to get a medical evaluation for autism which could give him more services in the future, and I see how that would be helpful. I no longer care about the possible negative effects of having a label or having all this testing included in his record. I care that both of my sons are healthy and happy, and I have learned that we are all neurodivergent in some ways, and our society has to become more understanding and accepting."

Fanny is helping to create a more loving, welcoming world through her open and inclusive attitudes. She is grateful now for the information she received from the specialists but still feels that the process could be made more compassionate. She is convinced that well-meaning professionals could be trained to acknowledge the feelings of parents and communicate difficult information in a more caring way. Her story brings up the important question of what compassionate collaboration between professionals and parents could look like in the future. In other words, how can parents and professionals collaborate in emotionally intelligent ways and use communication tools that create real understanding?

Ultimately, Fanny is so happy to have been part of a community of parents and teachers in the special education program dedicated to sharing perspectives of a child in caring ways. She didn't start out recognizing how important her collaboration with professionals was for Sean's development. Her ability to collaborate amplified when she was finally paired with someone she learned to trust, someone who taught her how to help Sean be successful and empowered her as a mom.

Reflective questions:

How does communicating authentically allow for better outcomes in any conversations with professionals?

Resources:

Siegel, Lawrence, JD, *The Complete IEP Guide: How to Advocate for Special Education Services for your Child*, Nolo, 2011.

Best Thing: Respect the Values of Co-Parenting Partners

"The fundamental law of human beings is interdependence. A person is a person through other persons."

Desmond Tutu

Bianca balances two households, three cultures, and two children, with a full-time career as a social worker, which she loves. Her busy life reflects the complexity of relationships in modern families. She and her partner, Ryan, are one of the 42 percent of families in our country that include a child from another marriage. Bianca plays the historically maligned role of stepmom, as she partners with Ryan and his former wife, Jen, to co-parent ten-year-old Ava. Bianca and Ryan also have a two-year-old son named Tavi. In addition, to the biological mix of their blended family, there is the challenge of integrating very different cultures. Bianca emigrated from Mexico at the age of six, and her extended family still lives there. Ryan's family is Navajo, and Ava's biological mom, Jen, is Korean.

Learning how to step-parent

Successfully navigating the complicated role of stepmother, especially one that involves cultural diversity, involves three things: 1) listening to the father about his values and vision of child-rearing; 2) getting to know the child over a long period of time; and 3) learning to co-parent with the child's biological mother, Jen. Bianca has managed to check all those boxes, but that doesn't mean it hasn't been challenging.

Bianca was 29 when she started dating Ryan, and she didn't realize at first that he had a two-year-old daughter. Since their relationship wasn't serious, Ryan didn't bring her into Ava's life, though Bianca met her occasionally for brief interactions. As she and Ryan grew closer, Bianca was extremely touched by watching his loving ways with his daughter. "At the time, I wasn't interested in becoming a mother, but when I watched Ryan with Ava, I was so impressed that I started thinking about what it would be like to be a mother myself. I loved children and had always been around them, but I liked my free and easy lifestyle at that point and wasn't thinking of settling down". Their relationship took time, and Bianca slowly fell in love with Ava as well as her dad.

Forming a gradual bond

Bianca found herself comforting Ava when she was missing her mom, Jen. At first, Bianca had felt judgmental of Jen, but she grew to respect the healthy, loving attachment Ava had with her. As we now know, psychologists feel it is crucially important for stepparents to respect and actively support a child's attachment to their biological parents. Bianca was also creating her own unique loving relationship with Ava, listening to her feelings, and spending time with her during visits to her and Ryan's. Both mothers eventually developed the belief that Ava was benefiting from getting love from both of them, but that big picture perspective took a long time to develop.

In fact, Bianca had avoided direct contact with Jen when she was first living with Ryan. First of all, they didn't know each other, and when they did, it felt awkward to see each other. Over time, Bianca started to see that it would help Ava if she communicated with Jen, and Bianca began texting Jen about things that came up. The communication allowed them to start collaborating regularly as alloparents to support Ava. "We weren't really friends, like we wouldn't hang out, but we definitely co-parented." Meanwhile, Bianca gave birth to Octavio, so Ava had a little brother, who was crazy about "his big sissy." Bianca's ability to collaborate with Jen provides an important role model for Ava and Tavi, who will encounter unfamiliar people in their lives and benefit from communicating with them.

Now there are apps for stepparents to communicate with biological parents, reflecting the advances in our technological age, but also the significant rise in blended families.

Honoring diverse family cultures

Bianca has also stepped up to bridge the cultural diversity in her family. She is a strong believer in keeping her Mexican heritage alive, and she has a created a home altar with pictures of her ancestors and honors them as part of the Día de loss Muertos celebration. Recently, Bianca asked Jen how to make Korean Kim-Chi, then went with Ava, bought the ingredients, and made a huge batch. She wants to celebrate the Korean culture equally in their home, as well as Ryan's Native American heritage.

Bianca and Ryan have chosen to live in a very diverse neighborhood, and Bianca talks proudly about the families on her block: an African American family, immigrants from Cambodia, and another from the Middle East. Bianca and Ryan talk to the children about honoring each of the cultures represented in their family, and they take the family to Native American pow-wows. As Ottavio now turns three, Bianca has located a Native American preschool for him to attend. Their family embodies the pluralistic ideal of a world where differences are embraced, and adults collaborate to raise their children in a way that fosters a sense of unity.

Reflective questions:

How does recognizing the love that exists in relationships help us to overcome judgment?

Resources:

Weiss, Diana, PhD, *Wisdom on Step-parenting: How to Succeed Where Others Fail*, CreateSpace Independent Publishing Platform, 2012.

Chapter Five: The Big Picture of Transforming Out-of-Control Behavior

"Mothers are the most vulnerable family members when it comes to the false belief that we can control our children ... The process of self-reflection, self-evaluation, and change is essentially self-loving and can't exist in an atmosphere of judgment and blame."

Anonymous

My parents were able to collaborate on many things in their marriage, but child discipline wasn't one of them. They could plan a budget to buy a new house or save for a vacation. But it never occurred to them to confer adult to adult about how to change their three children's behavior at the dinner table. During one period, they argued continually about my sister, brother, and me, on what my father considered our out-of-control behavior. As a ship's captain, he had strict ideas about how people should act at the dinner table, conditioned by his time at sea for months, having his meals with other ship's officers. My dad would get upset if he noticed me reading. (My father didn't approve of bringing books to the table. He probably would have also objected to the smartphone.) However, he had an even bigger reaction if he saw my brother reaching over and tussling with our little sister at the table.

When that happened, he would typically turn to my mom and say, "Look at what they're doing; they have no manners," his way of suggesting my mom was being too permissive. This was actually a type of patriarchal shaming reflecting society's beliefs that mothers should be able to raise perfectly behaved children. My mother often defended herself by saying that children learned manners through "role modeling." This was her gentle way of protesting my father's tendencies to yell at the table when he saw behavior he considered "out of control." They were at an impasse. You might ask, dear reader, why I kept sneaking a book to the table when I knew it would upset my father. I ask myself that question. But as someone who has written a book on child discipline and given hundreds of workshops on the subject, I have become an expert on the power of misguided attention.

99

I know that the more energy adults give to a negative behavior, the more likely it will be for children to repeat it. I also know that if partners in the home or in an educational environment don't find rules they can both agree on, children will keep testing to find out what the boundaries are. I found that principle illustrated in a recent interview, quoting Julia Roberts about the consistent effort she and her husband, Danny Moder, put into creating firm rules with their children, so they could present a united front. They never wanted their children to be able to play one parent off the other, so they emphasized family rules. In a time when everyone is on their phones, they had their children immediately leave their phones in individual charging stations when they got home from school, and no phones were ever allowed at the dinner table, so that family time would be uninterrupted. The kids are older now, but Julia and Danny felt that part of being unconditionally loving with them was uniting on firm guidelines.

Attention to the negative

Back to my family where few rules existed, I'm convinced that observing my parents' unproductive discussions gave me a preternatural interest in child discipline. At an early age, I realized that my brother, sister, and I never experienced any consequence for not complying with our dad's wishes for the kind of dinner table he had on the ship. We actually got a payoff for disobedience through the abundant attention he showered on us for misbehaving. If he had been able to step out of his upset and look at the big picture, he might have noticed that my brother, sister, and I demonstrated several positive behaviors at dinner time: coming to dinner on time, not complaining about the food, and clearing our plates afterward.

If my father had given us positive attention for the ways we were complying, he could have changed our dinner-time dynamics. However, he was focused on what he considered out-of-control behavior and on my mother's perceived failures to exercise control because it didn't meet his specifications. His disapproving energy was like fuel to our misbehaving fire.

My parents weren't alone in their discipline dilemmas. In a 2015 cross-cultural study of parents, 57% said they struggled to find the best ways to discipline, and 42% said they wished they didn't raise their voices or yell at their children.

Over the years, many books have been written on the subject of child discipline. I've written more than one of them myself. My book, *Who's in Control?* based on Diana Baumrind's groundbreaking research on the efficacy of parents being authoritative, rather than permissive or authoritarian, is still widely used. Most books on discipline, mine included, start with the basic premise that people need to collaborate on a few basic rules that children can understand. I have done countless workshops on bringing out the best in children. However, rather than simply detailing behavior management techniques in this chapter, I want to focus on how blaming mothers for children's behavior problems undermines their effectiveness and diminishes their sense of self-worth.

Shame about children's behavior

Over the years, one of the consistent emotions mothers have shared with me is shame related to their inability to manage a child's out-of-control behavior. The label out-of-control comes from the critical eye of the observer, in this case, my father, who couldn't see that his tirades were making our behavior worse. My mom felt ashamed that she couldn't coordinate a happy, harmonious dinner time without behavior problems and arguing. Her negative self-talk made her feel helpless, a crucial factor in persistent behavior issues that makes the problem seem unresolvable. If we want to bring out children's best selves, we need to let go of shame and guilt so we can see all the parts of the situation. We need a big picture.

The subject of shame and out-of-control behavior reminds me of another dinnertime story a young mother brought to me years ago. Mealtimes often present conundrums today when people's lives are busy, yet they want to have a pleasant sit-down meal together at the end of the day.

Jeanne, the mother of two little girls, came to see me in tears. She spoke in a faint voice as if someone might overhear her, even though we had complete privacy in my office. Jeanne told me about a problem she considered out-of-control. She couldn't imagine a resolution. Jeanne then confessed that she couldn't stop her four-year-old daughter, Olivia, from walking on the dinner table at night. No matter how many times she lifted Olivia down, the four-year-old would climb right back up.

One of the things I do when I consult with a parent is to try to get a big picture of the situation with all the variables at play. As I listened, I saw that Jeanne was actually overwhelmed with the whole process of preparing and serving dinner. She was in the process of teaching her younger daughter, Miriam, to sit at the table without a highchair, and it took lots of her attention. In the meantime, she was setting the table and serving the food. Her husband usually arrived late and might still be on his cell phone, and in the midst of the chaos, Olivia made her debut on the table. I felt like applauding Olivia's misbehavior because I could see that it was a way of capturing her mother's complete attention in a busy household. However, Jeannie didn't have the self-compassion to see how hard this situation was for her. It was actually her negative self-talk that made it seem hopeless. Her dilemma shows how crazy discipline situations can become when several factors are at play: a child getting a big reaction to a behavior and wanting to experience it again, and a mother feeling overwhelmed by having to multitask without a collaborator to help her see the big picture.

Jeanne's shame had kept her from telling anyone about the issue, and so she was isolated, blaming herself for having such an unusual problem. It seemed like no one would understand.

But I did understand. I sensed that Olivia was jealous of her younger sister. One of the issues I encounter over and over is that once a younger sibling arrives, the older child rarely gets time alone with the mom. For a young child, quality time alone with a parent is a powerful motivator. Olivia had learned that when she climbed on the table, she got her mom's whole attention and could pull her Jeannie's focus away from her younger sister.

Collaboration on discipline

Once Jeanne and her husband started working together, I advised them to give Olivia positive attention for all the ways she was complying. I also urged them to set up a regular time for Jeanne to be alone with Olivia for a predictable play time during the week. They also established a rule: no table climbing and a logical consequence for breaking it. If she climbed on the table even for a minute, Olivia had to leave dinner briefly until she was ready to sit with her family. The table walking went away, and years later, when I saw Jeanne, she told me how proud she was that her daughter, Olivia, had gotten a wonderful new job. She no longer remembered the phase when her daughter's behavior had seemed out of control, and she needed to collaborate with me in order to see the big picture for resolution.

One of the secrets of getting children to follow rules is to discuss them in a neutral way at a time when they aren't breaking them. Asking children what the rules should be in their house helps to get their buy-in with complying with them. Fortunately, today, new strength-based approaches to serious issues can be transformative in helping mothers step beyond shame and successfully handle problems that once seemed overwhelming.

A strength-based approach to out-of-control behavior

In the 1990s, Howard Glasser, a psychotherapist in Tucson, Arizona, found himself working with children in his private practice who were considered out-of-control by their parents and often by their schools. These children would usually be categorized as having conditions like attention deficit hyperactivity or oppositional defiance disorder, but Glasser dropped the labels and began describing his patients as "energy challenged."

As he collaborated with his clients, he challenged himself to see the positive aspects of their behavior, no matter how small. While they were still in his waiting room, he might comment on how quietly they were sitting or how respectfully they were handling the magazines, activities that would not typically draw praise. He felt an intuitive understanding of his clients because as a child he had persistently acted out for negative attention. He was convinced the adults in his life didn't understand him, and he often had problems at school.

Glasser began coaching parents and teachers to focus their energy on the tiniest examples of a child calming himself or complying with a request. He called this process "making miracles out of molecules," and it was so successful at healing relationships that he described his transformative results as *The Nurtured Heart Approach*. Glasser felt that conventional parenting techniques didn't work with intense children because they have a greater need for connection and are more sensitive to the environment. He began teaching parents and teachers to resist giving attention to negative behavior by lecturing, reprimanding, or yelling, and to focus instead on the smallest successes in sincere, heartfelt ways.

In 1999, he published *Transforming the Difficult Child* with Jennifer Easley, the first book to document his Nurtured Heart Approach (NHA), and he has published numerous books since then. The method doesn't operate through traditional techniques like trying to catch a child behaving. Instead, it coaches parents and teachers to observe positive elements of behavior that already exist but may have escaped their notice. The approach aims over time to change the child's self-perceptions, what Glasser calls a child's feeling of their own "greatness "and "inner wealth."

The approach teaches adults to take three unwavering stands: 1) refusing to give attention to negativity; 2) relentlessly energizing purposeful, positive behavior; and 3) setting clear rules and boundaries coupled with consequences. The Nurtured Heart Approach doesn't use punishment or time-outs. When a child breaks a rule, adults simply ask a child to "reset" themselves. The idea is to immediately get the child back "in the game" so adults give positive recognitions when the minute child shows self-control. After resetting, a child is welcomed back into the situation with no residual bad feelings about the previous behavior. After a transgression is addressed satisfactorily, every moment is considered brand new.

Many school districts across the country now teach the Nurtured Heart Approach to everyone on the staff who has contact with the children: administrators, teachers, cafeteria workers, and bus drivers. The goal is to have everyone encourage children by focusing on what children are doing right.

The power of the reset

Mothers can apply many of the same techniques employed in the Nurtured Heart Approach to pay attention to the big picture of their own lives and all that they are doing well. Focusing on the molecules of what they are doing right every day can prevent the negative spiral of worry and guilt. One of the most effective tools of NHA is the quick reset when an adult reminds a child to reset and then comments right away when they correct their behavior. This is a powerful tool for mothers to restore their own equilibrium. A mother can role model accountability by acknowledging her own mistakes or negative attitudes in the moment, and telling a child, "I need to reset myself." Resetting allows a mother to take care of herself and quickly realign with her values, rather than leaking negative feelings about herself or her child into other situations.

When parents take a strength-based approach to collaborating about discipline, they can validate each other's feelings of frustration but also recognize when their partner has handled a situation well. By looking at the big picture together, they can strategize to give each other needed breaks and help each other see increments of progress over time.

Mothers can also offer needed support to one another by recognizing each other's patience and creative problem-solving.

Here are some strategies to create positive behavior and harmony:

- Offer empathy to children for big feelings.

- Create rules with your child and write them down.

- Notice all the ways a child complies with rules and shows kindness to others.

- Understand developmental limitations; two-year-olds don't know how to share; three-year-olds are just learning words for feelings.

- Avoid describing behavior as "out of control" even in your own mind. Tell yourself you haven't found a way of resolving it yet.

- Collaborate with people to give positive attention to children and help them to recognize their own positive attributes and greatness.

- Take a strength-based approach with your partner, your alloparents, and promote a caring community. Note what others are doing right.

- Talk to yourself in kind ways, noticing your successes and appreciating loving moments with your child.

- Let go of shame about yourself, your child, and your co-collaborators. You are all learners.

- Look for the big picture to see all the hidden reasons a behavior might be occurring, like jealousy of a sibling or stress about a school transition.

- Understand the power of setting up even short, predictable times alone with your child.

- Listen to and empathize with your child's feelings, even as you set limits.

The ability of mothers to feel satisfied with their own efforts at adjusting a child's behavior is integral to maintaining positive influences in their children's lives. The next chapter explores the important role mothers play in picking up on and preventing bullying and exclusion.

Reflective questions:

What was discipline like in your family growing up?

Do you have a different perspective on shaping behavior than your parents?

Do you and your partner agree?

Resources:

Ausburn, Debbie, JD, and Ford, Natalie, PhD, *Raising Other People's Children, What Foster Parenting Taught Me about Bringing Together a Blended Family,* Harleigh Press, 2021.

Brown, Brené, *Women and Shame,* 3C Publishing, May 2004.

Easley, Jennifer, *Relationship Reset: Igniting Fierce Love for Couples using the Nurtured Heart Approach,* Nurtured Heart Publications, 2013.

Faber, Adele, and Mazlish, Elaine, *How to Talk so Children Will Listen and Listen so Children Will Talk.* Harper's Collins Reprint, 2002.

Glasser, Howard, *Notching It Up,* Nurturing Light Design, 2011.

Glasser, Howard, Easly, Jennifer, *Transforming the Difficult Child, The Nurtured Heart Approach,* Center for the Difficult Child, 1999.

Isaacs, Susan, *Who's in Control?* Perigee, 1986.

Kennedy, Becky, PhD, *Good Inside, A Guide to Becoming the Parent You Want to Be,* Harper Wave, September 2022.

Kohl, Isaacs Susan, *The Best Things Mothers Do,* Conari, 2004.

Mason, Erica, Gerald, "Julia Roberts Reveals the One Strict Rule She Has for Her Kids," Parade, September 11, 2025.

Here are the stories:

The four women in this chapter have quite different circumstances and represent the wide array of challenging behaviors mother's encounter.

In the first story, Betsy's son Daniel had a difficult adjustment returning to school after remote learning during COVID-19. After school, he started having daily tantrums about every little frustration. After talking to his teacher, Betsy was able to see the big picture of his perfectionism and give him the skills he needed to self-calm and reach out to others successfully.

The second story provides a different kind of role model. Debbie Arbuson has been a foster mother and a stepmother. She cares deeply about the teenagers who live with her, no matter how temporarily, and helps them stabilize by doing chores that contribute to the whole household. She also uses logical consequences when they don't follow the rules. Debbie illustrates how we can all discipline more effectively when we don't take a child's misbehavior personally.

The third story opens our eyes to the very difficult situations, mothers of children with special needs can experience. Kate Swenson has been an influential blogger and speaker supporting mothers with special needs children and working to change society's attitudes towards children with developmental issues. She and her husband have three children, and her oldest son, Cooper, was diagnosed with autism when he was three. When he began hurting his younger brother with no provocation, she began worrying about whether Cooper would have to leave their family to go to a group home. Then her mother-in-law made a suggestion that would transform their lives.

The fourth story allows us to witness the kind of miraculous transformations that can come from the Nurtured Heart Approach. As a school psychologist with two children of her own, Sarah felt eminently capable of adding two more children to her family who needed help. However, she quickly realized her confidence in her own abilities was naïve. Her foster children's behavior turned out to be so out-of- control that she and her husband worried that they would have to give them back to the state. That's when she discovered NHA at a seminar, and it changed her family's life. Sarah has given a TED Talk on the subject and now speaks to audiences around the world.

Best Thing: Notice Molecules of Self-Control

"At its root, perfectionism isn't really a deep love of being meticulous. It's about fear. Fear of making a mistake. Fear of disappointing others. Fear of Failure. Fear of success."

Michael Law

During COVID-19, Betsy's two boys, eight and five, had a tough time staying home all day, confined to remote learning. There was a lot of fighting between the two boys, and Betsy finally told them she was going to teach them a mindfulness technique called "Name it and Tame It." Every time there was a conflict, she insisted that they stop and talk about their feelings before negotiating a solution. This method of coaching, developed by Dr. Daniel Siegel, was a good stress reducer for Betsy's family.

However, when the COVID isolation was over and the boys returned to regular school, Betsy saw that re-entering the classroom was difficult for both of them socially. It was especially hard for her younger son, Daniel, and as time went by, her concerns only increased. A pattern started to develop, and when Daniel returned from school every day, he started having tantrums when the slightest thing didn't go his way.

A new pattern of blow-ups

His piano lessons on Zoom were often the scene for daily breakdowns. Although his piano teacher was encouraging and patient, the minute Daniel made a mistake playing, he threw a tantrum. He also had meltdowns when he couldn't have something, or when his older brother had friends visiting and he wasn't immediately included. Betsy could have approached his blowups sternly with threats, then consequences, but she realized Daniel was under stress and needed support; she just didn't know why.

As a result, Betsy made an appointment with his teacher and was surprised to hear that Daniel never fell apart at school. She discovered that the opposite was true. The teacher said Daniel followed the rules perfectly at school and was, in fact, one of her best-behaved students, but when Betsy asked if Daniel interacted well with the other students at recess, the teacher said he spent most of the time by himself.

The stress of perfection

Betsy realized that after reentering school post-COVID, Daniel's nervousness had made him a rule follower at school, holding in all his feelings then letting them out in bursts at home. He was like a pressure cooker by the time he got home, and Betsy wanted to help him learn to talk about his feelings instead of acting them out.

Since Betsy was still working from home, she was able to start paying close attention to all his reactions as soon as he came in the door in the afternoon. In the big picture, she felt that if she didn't intervene to help Daniel develop self-regulation skills at home, it could affect his whole life. She knew that he perpetually felt bad about himself, and after having a meltdown, he would put himself down through negative self-talk for having a tantrum.

When a child develops a pattern of reacting with anger, it's easy to get frustrated and lecture them about their lack of self-control. That typically makes the behavior worse because the adult is giving the child negative energy that amplifies the problems rather than connecting with the child and offering support.

Intervention before the tantrum

That was the pattern that was happening before Betsy started changing her own responses. She had previous training in giving helpful attention to any sign of positive behavior. She asked herself how she could give positive energy to Daniel before he had a meltdown. Betsy thought ahead about what caused his reactions so she could respond proactively. She started giving him praise for small facets of his behavior several times a day, saying, "I notice you're having big feelings right now, but you're breathing and staying calm." She explains, "I really laid it on thick. I took every opportunity to intervene *before* he fell apart." Soon, Daniel started turning to her and saying, "Look, Mom, I'm breathing." After a while, rather than just asking for her approval, he began taking natural, calming breaths.

Betsy got the whole family to collaborate with her. She talked to her husband, Cooper, Daniel's brother Sam, and his grandparents, and everyone was on board with giving Daniel positive feedback for calming himself. Consequently, Daniel's behavior began to transform. As his stress diminished, he began to open up to others socially as well.

Betsy had always known that Daniel was an empathic child, and she started trying to help to join in with his brother Sam's friends when they were over. "Daniel has a huge imagination and loves to entertain himself through fantasy. But I noticed that if they didn't respond well to his suggestions for play, he would come away crying." Betsy coached him to go back to the person who didn't immediately accept his idea and share his feelings, "The way you reacted to my idea really hurt my feelings." Sam's friends were older and would always apologize and make an attempt to include him.

Then Betsy talked to Daniel about school and how he might share his imaginary ideas with other children and play successfully. This coaching with Daniel about how to initiate play at home and at school started making him feel more confident, and he began reaching out to other children. Betsy was delighted that over a few months; he developed several friendships.

Empowerment to create change

Betsy is full of gratitude for all the collaboration she received and the good results. The whole family is thrilled to see Daniel express all his imagination, sensitivity, and compassion with his friends. Betsy could have taken Daniel's negative reactions personally and gotten into daily power struggles, sending him on time out for having a tantrum or habitually lecturing him.

Instead, she looked at the big picture and felt empowered to make a difference. Betsy didn't assume that Daniel's overreactions were just part of his personality; she believed that she could bring out more harmonious ways of responding that would serve him all his life.

Reflective questions:

What is the value of stepping back to observe a child's behavior rather than reacting in the moment?

Resources:

Siegel, Daniel, MD, *Whole- Brain Child: 12 Revolutionary Strategies to Nurture Your Child's Developing Mind,* Delacorte, 2011.

Best Thing: Use Logical Consequences

"Never take a child's limit-pushing personally."

Janet Lansbury

Debbie Ausburn has learned not to react to children's out-of-control behavior with intensity. As a foster mother, stepmom, and grandmother, she has helped children through loss and trauma and successfully supported them while they juggle problematic relationships with their biological families. Her core methods are loving sensitivity, stable routines, and reasonable expectations. Debbie listens to their stories and all their feelings about situations, comforts them about not being able to be with the people they love, and grounds them by teaching them important life skills.

Debbie is the queen of logical consequences and rarely shows any upset when implementing them. The children in her house are expected to do chores, and she constantly lets them know how valuable their help is. When older children skip their chores, the logical consequence is that they can't go out with their friends until their chores are done. Younger children can't watch TV until they complete their jobs.

Using a neutral tone

Debbie's effectiveness in using consequences is in her neutrality and ability to implement them with very few words. She knows that if she acts upset while giving a consequence, the situation will turn into a power struggle. So, she never lectures children about learning to be responsible; it's the consequence of missing out on something that helps them remember.

The examples in her book are extremely helpful. When one of the children forgot to take the garbage out, she quietly placed the bag of garbage in his room to take out the next day. One of the young boys in her care fell in love with her dogs and was excited about feeding them. She let him take on that responsibility, but as is so common with young children, he soon lost interest. Debbie didn't say anything and resumed taking care of the pets herself. But the boy noticed that the dogs weren't coming to him anymore, and Debbie commented that dog's bond with the person feeding them, which made him resume his tasks.

She has assigned everyone in the house to a laundry day. If a child misses their day, they have to wait to wash their clothes until the following week. The system keeps them from complaining about not having clean clothes, and they learn that their excuses for procrastinating do not change the situation.

Debbie puts great energy into infusing a sense of belonging for each child. Her message is always, "You are a valued part of this family, and we welcome and need you." She collaborates with them on decorating their bedrooms, allows them to choose the paint color, and works together to create a budget for linens and decorations. Older children get to help paint their room and are allowed to find a corner of the room to write their name.

Creating their own private space

Debbie allows teenagers to make their room a private space where no one will intrude. However, they are not allowed to bring food into their rooms, and one of the humorous ways that Debbie enforces consequences for doing so is by letting her beagle go into their rooms and eat the crumbs of their contraband food. Teenagers complain about the dog invading their space, but she says," Then don't bring food into your room."

Debbie has the complicated challenge of supporting her foster children through hurtful situations with their biological families. One thing she has learned is never to disparage a biological parent, no matter how disturbed she is by an adult's actions. Debbie wants the kids in her care to have loving relationships with their families, so rather than criticizing their parents, she responds neutrally. For instance, when a child asks her why her biological mom would do the things she's doing, she says, "I don't know. There are many possible reasons, but none of them have anything to do with you."

Preventing power struggles

She loves the children she cares for and knows they often are not happy about being in her home. She is able to maintain the big picture and not take it personally, even when they are angry and rejecting her.

Occasionally, she will get mad when they've done something really unsafe and make an exaggerated declaration, "You're grounded until you're 35." However, the young people know that she's concerned about them and will come up with a reasonable consequence the next morning.

Using consequences instead of lecturing not only prevents power struggles, but it also allows children to have a sense of the adult world and the kinds of attitudes and skills they will need to independently manage their lives successfully. It's interesting in this regard that Debbie stays in touch with her foster children and often responds to requests for emotional support long after they have left her care. They come back to her because, in her words and actions, she has shown that she cares deeply about them and will help them handle the challenges that come their way.

When the subject of child discipline comes up, we automatically think of parents with their biological children. But Debbie presents a role model for caring about and supporting any child who comes into our lives. Like Debbie, relatives, teachers, coaches, caregivers all have responsibilities to learn non-reactive, strength-based approaches that bring out children's best qualities. Our umbrella of caring needs to include all children, as well as their parents, as we develop practical tools together to create a more compassionate society.

Reflective questions:

How does Debbie's story highlight the value of being able to set rules and consequences neutrally rather than taking children's behavior personally?

Resources.

Ausburn, Debbie, 2021, *Raising Other People's Children,* Hatherleigh Press, 2021.

Best Thing: Let Go of Shame

*"There are countless forces beyond your control
that affect how your child behaves."*

Harriet Lerner, PhD

Kate Swenson was standing in a grocery store just a few years after her son Cooper had been diagnosed with autism and overheard a customer berating the slowness of a young man with special needs bagging groceries. He muttered, "I don't have all day to wait for these retards." Before Kate could say anything, other people in the line justly confronted him for his ignorance and cruelty. In that moment, Kate vowed to change the world not only for her own son, but for all special needs children and their families. She hoped that someday Cooper would be able to work in the world, and it was agonizing to think that the world might not accept him.

As a result, she soon started giving public talks on behalf of those with disabilities and their families. She focused on getting people "to open their eyes to differences, and ultimately to be kind." She visited the state capitol in St. Paul, Minnesota, and spoke with the governor and senator, made phone calls, wrote letters, and started a blog called *Finding Cooper's Voice.*

Trying to normalize her son's differences

Kate feels passionate about her mission to educate people and open their hearts. "I shared Cooper. I shared his wins and his struggles. I shared his sounds, his hoarding, his joy, his anxiety. I did everything I could to normalize his differences in hopes that I would reach that awful man from the grocery store and every person like him."

Mothers like Kate, who are willing to share honest stories about everyday life, help to remove the shame they so often feel when their child's behavior is objectionable to others. In her book, *Forever Boy, Kate* documented the endless hours she spent every day, starting at 4 a.m., following Cooper through their house as he emptied drawers, piled bathroom items into the tub and moved from room to room, making a mess. Cooper never stopped this routine from early morning until he went to bed at 8 p.m. In addition, there were sporadic out-of-control tantrums when Kate would hold Cooper to prevent him from banging his head on the floor and hurting himself. Instead, Cooper would bang his head on Kate's chest, and she would whisper "I love you" over and over to try to calm him. For years, that was a daily experience, but then it suddenly got worse.

Dealing with out-of-control aggression

It happened when Cooper was eight and the tantrums took a scary turn. One day, Cooper suddenly attacked his six-year-old brother Sawyer. When other instances of aggression occurred, Kate took the precaution of having her two younger sons lock themselves in her office until Cooper's tantrum stopped. But this began a spiral of worry about whether she would be able to keep her younger boys safe. Would she have to send her younger children away or would she need to put Cooper in a group home? From the time of his diagnosis at three, Kate had hoped she would be able to cure Cooper of his autism so that these questions might never arise. Now she realized that her family hadn't been spared from these possibilities, and his behavior was getting more out of control.

Then, just as her life seemed to be at a tipping point, Kate got some unexpected help. One night, when the family was visiting her in-laws, her mother-in-law, a retired nurse, said, "Cooper is so unhappy. I think it's time you tried medication. He needs some peace." Kate had never considered medication. She saw medicating children as a sign of failure. However, she was fearful that one of her children could be hurt, and she couldn't imagine another way forward.

Observing surprising transformations

She called Cooper's doctor, then broke the appointment, then called again and finally got the medication. Shortly after Cooper started taking the medication, Kate and her husband saw a dramatic change. One morning, when they came into the living room, they found Cooper peacefully sitting on the couch, something they had never witnessed in the past. There were other remarkable changes. Cooper had always been non-verbal, but after a few weeks, he started saying words. He also seemed happy, and his aggression disappeared. He even started sharing a bed with his younger brother.

Although his changes seemed miraculous, Kate is quick to say she doesn't think medication is the answer for everyone and that each parent of a special needs child is on their own journey. What mothers do need, Kate stresses, is understanding and compassion She wants people to be aware that having a child with special needs can include lifelong grief for all the things that they will never do.

One day while chatting with one of her co-workers, one of them jumped up and imitated a child with autism flapping their hands. Some of her colleagues later apologized to her for this woman's insensitivity, but though they couldn't understand just how hurtful this was for Kate. Seeing Cooper flap his hands in excitement was actually touching for her because it usually meant he was happy.

Kate never knew if she was changing the attitudes of people who didn't have a person with special needs in their lives, until one day, she got an email from a woman in her seventies who lives in the South. The woman said she knew nothing of autism until she read her stories about Cooper. Even though she was fascinated and touched by them, the woman admitted that she was confused by why Cooper acted the way he did. She told Kate that one day, she had seen a grown man at a local store covering his ears and flapping his hands and making strange sounds. The woman said she immediately thought of Kate's blog about Cooper and felt protectiveness to him. When a few women in the store started criticizing the man for being loud, the woman said she had also pointed out their unkindness and lack of understanding.

Reading the story of that elderly woman's transformation from ignorance to advocacy helped Kate to feel in her own small way that she was accomplishing the goal she had from the moment Cooper was first diagnosed. "If I can educate one unknowing person and remove people's fear of neurodivergence then I am doing the right thing."

Changing her own attitude toward autism

Mothers like Kate, who share their day- to- day stories that include stresses and resentments as well as love and joy will help create a world where success isn't measured by good grades, graduations, promotions, or salaries but by our abilities to accept and embrace every aspect of the human journey. Kate started out thinking that having faith in her herself meant that she would automatically be able to handle any of her child's behavior, but eventually she learned humility and the willingness to listen to others.

Reflective questions:

How can we all work to overcome our inherited belief that people with special needs are "less than" others?

Resources:

Swenson, Kate, *Forever Boy,* Parker Row, 2022.

Best Thing: Scrutinize For Success

"If you can feel one single speck of magnificence in yourself or another, nothing stands in the way of that flame."

Howard Glasser, creator of the Nurtured Heart Approach®

Sarah How remembers lying in bed one night, crying and telling herself, "You are a complete disaster as a mother." As a school psychologist, she felt supremely equipped to handle children who needed help. The previous year, she, her husband, Mark, and their children, Justin, 9, and Lydia, 3, were inspired to adopt 12-year-old Kalob, and his 6-year-ld half-sister, Chloe, who had been found living in a meth_house. However, Sarah hadn't realized that her professional skill in communicating clear rules and consequences would not work with severely traumatized kids.

Living in constant chaos

Life in their suddenly expanded family meant that the day typically started with trying to get the children to school. Sarah was working full-time, so Mark was in charge of driving the children. Sometimes, Kalob would refuse to get out of the car, and Mark would have to physically lift him onto the sidewalk in front of the middle school and drive away. The evenings were filled with power struggles. At dinner time, Kalob and Chloe would often refuse to come to the dinner table. If Sarah raised her voice to insist that they come, Kalob would yell back at her. Moreover, their interaction would sometimes trigger a memory of trauma, and he would lie on the floor in a fetal position and talk in a baby voice. As for his half-sister Chloe, she was so insecure that Sarah had to carry her around the house or at least stay close to her much of the time.

The whole family lived in a state of constant disruption, and every day felt more defeating. To their horror, Sarah and Mark found themselves whispering, "Do you think this whole adoption thing is working?" They took turns answering, "No." It was painful to admit they were failing, but their logical minds couldn't find a way to move forward. If Kalob and Chloe couldn't follow any reasonable rules, how could their situation work? They prayed for guidance, but they also scheduled a meeting of the social work team to arrange to stop the adoption if things didn't get better. Then, suddenly, Sarah felt their prayers were answered when she heard about a new way of creating positive behavior.

Attending a positive workshop

Sarah's special education director sent her to an August workshop designed to help professionals and parents "transform the behavior of challenging children." It was called The Nurtured Heart Approach.. Sarah had never heard of it, and she entered the seminar fatigued and despondent. But after listening to the speaker for an hour, she excitedly texted Mark, "I think we have hope!" The Nurtured Heart Approach suggested that Sarah start out by not complaining about her home situation to others, but to learn to talk about it in a completely different way. Before attending the workshop, Sarah constantly cited all the negative things going on with the children to anyone who would listen. "Can you believe this?" she would ask, citing some outrageous behaviors guaranteed to get her sympathy. The Nurtured Heart Approach insisted that she start noticing and telling others about the tiniest things in her home that were going right. This admonition started to shift her whole perspective. "I started scrutinizing our home life for small successes."

The Nurtured Heart's emphasis on focusing on the positive allowed Sarah to zoom out of her brain's negative bias and step into the big picture to discover that some of Kalob and Chloe's behaviors were actually okay and potentially helpful. "I focused on little moments of success like Kalob bringing his plate to the sink after dinner. Even if it didn't get to the dishwasher, at least he didn't leave the plate on the table".

Learning to reset herself

After a few short months of immersing themselves in following the new approach, Sarah and Mark made an about-face and told the social work team that they were going through with the adoption. It was finalized on November 11, 2009, the National Day of Adoption.

One of the cornerstones of the approach is calmly asking children to "reset" their behavior when they break a rule rather than repeating the rule and raising your voice. This was a huge change for Sarah. "I was a yeller, but when I was about to yell, I started trying to reset myself by focused breathing. The kids would say, "Mom's breathing." Her daughter, Lydia, commented one day, "We don't yell at our house anymore!" and it was then that Sarah realized that she had been part of the problem. She was learning to self-regulate and teaching her children to regulate themselves at the same time.

She decided to fly to Arizona and immerse herself in a week-long training, and after that, Sarah attended another training and became a Certified Advanced Trainer who could help other families like hers. She got to know Howie Glasser the creator of the approach, and she ended up doing a TEDx Fargo talk called, "Igniting Greatness: Using the Nurtured Heart Approach".

The training enabled Sarah not only to love her adopted children but also to support them in ways that actually helped them. For instance, because of past trauma, Chloe initially couldn't stand to hear anything positive about herself. Sarah worked around that by keeping a daily greatness journal about Chloe. One day, after a massive tantrum, Chloe wrote, "I hate you." in the journal. Sarah says, "It was a holy spirit moment because I got the chance to respond, "I will always love you and always be your mom."

Becoming a force to help others

Sarah sees their whole family journey as a gift from God. "I had to completely give up thinking I could manage the adoption. I had to surrender and ask God to take over, and my prayers were answered. It was then that I heard about the Nurtured Heart Approach. God gave me tools, and I took them." As a result, Sarah has become someone known for her ability to help parents and convince them they don't have to give up or feel like failures. By looking at the big picture and widening their perspective, they can learn concrete ways to nurture success.

The How family has done well. Kalob is now a chef in a restaurant, Justin is a videographer, Chloe is a special education paraprofessional for preschool and kindergarten, and Lydia is attending college for Marketing and Global Business.

Reflective questions:

How can a parent switch their mind-set to focus on what's going right?

How does venting perpetuate problems in our own minds?

Resources:

How, Sarah, "Igniting Greatness: The Nurtured Heart Approach," 8.38, TED X Fargo, 2013/ https://youtu.be/9lXNl8NpyuY

How, Sarah, *Mission Greatness Spy,* How2 Creative Services, 2025,

Chapter Six: The Big Picture of Preventing Bullying and Exclusion

"Children are our future, and their mothers are its guardians."

Former United Nations Secretary General, Kafi Annan

When my son, Matt, was two, he had a playmate who loved to grab his toys and run away. This isn't unusual behavior for a toddler, but I wanted Matt to learn to stick up for himself, so I started role-playing with him. I initiated an imaginary game with stuffed animals. I would pretend my animal was talking to his, Then I would playfully tug his animal while coaching him to say, "No, that's mine!"

As soon as Matt demanded his toy back, I returned it and praised him for speaking up. This was my first attempt to prevent a gentle child from being bullied by others. I could have blamed the other child, but I focused on building Matt's social skills. Psychotherapist and bullying expert, Ronald Mah, agrees. In his book, *Getting Beyond Bullying and Exclusion,* he says that teaching a child to get a toy back from another child is a foundation for developing the confidence to assert themselves..

An ideal of friendship

At two, Matt and I could begin talking about how our family wanted to treat others and have them treat us. This was the beginning of many discussions about friendship. Not being bullied by another two-year-old was tier one, but I also wanted Matt to develop empathy, to include others, and to be able to problem-solve when there were disagreements. I wanted him to learn to be a good friend, an ally, a person who would stick up for others, and be a creator of understanding. I wanted the same for my daughters, Gabrielle and Mari.

These were noble aspirations that seemed simple when my children were young, and I was able to pick their playmates. As my kids grew older, periodic challenges appeared. In addition, to the many rewards of friendship, there were sometimes hurt feelings to assuage, exclusions to understand, and unhealthy influences to counteract as well as parents who had different values and limits for their children. And when my children's feelings were hurt or they felt excluded, I experienced pain too. That was part of the process of supporting their growth and my own.

The pivotal role of mothers

My heart goes out to mothers who are typically the ones tracking their children's relationships, the ones trying to help them cope with hurt feelings and social challenges. Research shows that fathers are also important in their children's social development. But, in the structure of American society, moms are usually the significant ones holding the big picture of their children's social-emotional experiences across settings, and for the most part, they do that without a road map.

If you have a child, dear reader, I urge you to believe in your abilities to aid their social development and to feel compassion for yourself when you don't have ready-made answers to the challenges they experience. I hope you notice everything you are doing right because I've seen over and over the pivotal role mothers play in helping their children to develop social skills and handle conflicts. Today, they are typically the ones who tune into their children's need for support and find creative ways to help them through stressful social situations. But it wasn't always that way.

A life-changing incident

When I was growing up, adults didn't typically concern themselves with children's friendships. Kids played outside most of the time with minimal adult supervision. No one in my life at home or at school expressed concerns about kids bullying one another. They didn't coach me about what I should do if someone singled me out for taunting. Maybe that's because I'm white and don't have a disability, so I had the privilege of not sticking out as different in my non-diverse, middle-class neighborhood. Of course, there were cliques and exclusions between girls in my high school, but that was considered normal. I didn't know then that those hierarchies in girls' relationships can be a form of bullying.

Then one day, I witnessed bullying between boys first-hand. While walking home from school, I came upon a group of teenage boys teasing another boy who had special needs. They may have called him a "retard;" a common taunt in those days. When I spotted them, they had circled around the boy on a street corner near a crosswalk, and they were keeping him from crossing the street. Without thinking, I stepped into the group, yelled at the teenage boys to stop the teasing, and helped him move away from them. Then, I introduced myself and learned that his name was Bruce and that he went to my high school. I had never seen him before because he was in a special education program tucked out of sight from the rest of us, since that was before mainstreaming. No one ever talked to us about special needs or how to treat people who learned differently. But it didn't take a background in special education for me to understand that I was observing a young person going through a potential trauma. Later, I helped him get home and talked to his mom about the incident.

Watching those teens teasing someone who had a hard time articulating his distress, had an impact on me and made me want to understand more about bullying. I didn't know the boys personally, but I could see they enjoyed messing with someone who seemed vulnerable. I could surmise, even at the time, that they gained social status with each other by exerting power. Surprisingly, I provided a quick intervention by simply asking them, "What are you thinking? and pointing to Bruce's frightened expression. Suddenly, they were no longer a cohesive group, just a bunch of boys who looked confused themselves. I didn't have to shame them or label them as bullies; I wanted to help them to see a bigger picture, one that included Bruce's feelings. It was my first experience of being an ally.

A focus on prevention

In *Getting Beyond Bullying and Exclusion, Pre K-5,* Ronald Mah offers many examples of kids bullying or excluding those they perceive as different or vulnerable with an emphasis on strategies for teaching them more self-control and empathy. He offers an equal number of practical tools for supporting children who need to step out of the victim role and assert themselves. Part of that process is understanding what bullying is. Today bullying has become a hot topic, and people often worry that their child is being bullied whenever they have an argument that turns physical with another child.

Definitions of bullying

Parents are understandably concerned when their child gets hurt, and they often come to me worried that their child is a victim of bullying. I try to help them calmly assess their child's interactions and the role the child tends to play in conflicts. It's developmentally typical for young children to have disagreements. Before they learn to express their frustrations in words, they may lose control and shove or hit each other, and adults have to intervene. These behaviors should disappear as they learn the basic social skill of asking for what they need through words rather than actions.

The red flag that indicates a situation may involve bullying is the existence of a pattern. Bullying is defined as repeated, aggressive behavior involving a real or perceived power imbalance between an older, bigger, or more popular child's physical or verbal aggression against a smaller one. Bullying occurs when a person or a group targets someone smaller, more vulnerable, or less popular. Bullying is defined as a pattern of targeted behavior.

It might involve name calling, taunting, or threats of violence. With girls it more often happens through exclusion or spreading rumors. That's called relational bullying and includes patterns like not answering another girl when she talks or walking away when she wants to connect.

When I was growing up, the field of social/emotional learning was in its infancy. Today, psychologists know more about bullying and the ways parents and teachers can ameliorate it by teaching children social skills and developing their emotional intelligence. That process often begins with mothers because, as noted, they tend to be the person most aware of their children's social interactions across different settings.

Parents as emotional coaches

Mothers' concerns with bullying often start with their children's complaints. Moms are the usual recipients of reports about upsets with other children. In the preschool and elementary years, children start to develop the ability to verbalize their frustrations with social interactions, and mothers usually hear about disturbances when they pick them up from school or daycare. Children's stories can sound dramatic and are often hard for a parent to evaluate without input from teachers. A child may say, "Jessie wouldn't play with me, and I was alone the whole day." However, the teacher may point out that the complaining child was in fact able to find others to play with when their best friend was with someone else.

Hearing about a child feeling left out can be a personal trigger for mothers since all of us have experienced rejection and exclusion at some point and naturally want to protect our children from feeling rejected. However, research shows that if a mother can listen and validate a child's feelings without jumping in with a remedy like, "You should just find another friend," the child's stress is lowered, and they can develop confidence about solving problems with friends. We want children to have the chance to experience their emotions and think about what they want to do next. Furthermore, when mothers listen and learn about the situation without providing solutions, it builds trust so children will communicate about future upsets. Discussing social situations also helps parents tune into children's relationships that are going awry and try to prevent unhealthy social patterns. However, parents need support when they try to make changes in a child's problematic ways of interacting whether the child is typically impulsive and aggressive or lacking in confidence. It takes positive collaboration to bring about change.

Remedies for aggression

Let's start with the aggressive child. Mothers will usually hear about a problem with their child being aggressive when a teacher contacts them that their child has hurt someone with or without provocation. A mother may also witness her child expressing anger physically toward a friend. It's often hard for parents to know whether a behavior is problematic or just part of a stage. When mothers get reports of a child hurting others, it can be embarrassing, and mothers may blame themselves for having a child who acts out in anger. It's also tempting to blame the other child and claim that they are a negative influence. Hearing from the school that a teacher a child needs more support to learn self-control can begin the collaboration process, so they can work together to bring about change. Parents can help each other by holding positive attitudes towards children who have problematic behavior. In these situations, the parents and the child need support.

Interactions that teach social skills

Adults help active, impulsive children by holding the perspective that they are learners. We want to avoid labelling highly active children as aggressors or bullies and instead concentrate on helping them learn how to regulate their behavior and understand other people's feelings. We want the children themselves to believe they are capable of being kind, caring friends to others.

Changing impulsive behavior works best as a multi-pronged approach. Children need clear rules and expectations, and it's confusing to them if guidelines are applied inconsistently or vary from situation to situation. For example, if hitting or name-calling is tolerated at home or conversely, reacted to with intensity, it's often hard for children to curb those reactions in other settings like school. Children often become addicted to the negative attention they get when they act out, and if we want children to learn self-control, we need to learn how to react with neutral authority when they make mistakes. Strong reactions from adults stimulate children to act out more.

Situations that involve hitting or teasing are often perfect opportunities to teach social skills, The adult can start by calmly reminding the child of the rule, "No hitting" but can also ask the child to notice how his or her playmate or sibling is feeling in the moment. Noticing and interpreting social cues like facial expressions is a central aspect of emotional intelligence and recognizing that someone is hurt is the first step in acquiring the ability to make amends.

Calming techniques

Children who are impulsive also need to learn how to calm themselves physically and emotionally. The inability to control their impulses is a consistent characteristic of children who bully. One effective way self-control is learned is through games. This brings us to the often-neglected subject of fathers and the important ways they engage with children. Fathers typically play with children differently than mothers and often receive criticism because the games they play often stimulate arousal. However, research shows that there is an evolutionary aspect to a father's arousal play that encourages children to gain impulse control. When children get excited during a running or roughhousing game and suddenly have to stop, their bodies learn important lessons in self-control Psychologists call the ability to self-calm and control one's impulses "self-regulation."

Traditionally, mothers have also played games that promote self-control and turn-taking, such as "Simon Says," "Mother May I," or "Red-Light Green Light". Again, when children learn to quickly stop, freeze, and exercise self-control, they are gradually able to extend those abilities to other social situations. In fact, those games are so effective with young children that child and occupational therapists often use them in social skills groups.

Mothers also foster self-regulation in highly active children by consistently asking them to pause and breathe to calm themselves when they're upset. It's also true that parents with highly active children often boost their own skills by learning about sensory integration activities. In addition, other physical activities like running or doing heavy work like carrying big bags of groceries or pushing hard against a wall can help ground and calm a child. When we concentrate on helping children calm their sensory systems, we are less likely to feel helpless or frustrated with them.

Mothers of highly active children need support

Again, moms who have children who are considered aggressive or have been labeled as bullies need understanding and support rather than blame. When other parents gossip about a classmate who is trying to learn self-control, it not only undermines the child's ability to see themselves in new ways, but it can also affect a classroom or team's ability to function as a caring community. It takes patience and perseverance for parents and teachers to work together to help a highly reactive child to learn to express emotions in socially appropriate ways.

In addition, reactive children need positive feedback when they demonstrate self-regulation and empathy. In a two-year study at the University of Arizona, psychotherapist Howard Glasser, the founder of the Nurtured Heart Approach, taught parents to avoid negative reactions to children's behavior, to acknowledge times when they demonstrated self-control and consideration for others, and provide clear limits. The results of this study showed a reduction in impulsive behaviors.

Furthermore, research shows that mothers can help both highly active children and those who need to be more assertive through an important process called "emotional coaching." This approach involves listening empathically and validating a child's feelings, even when the cause of the upset seems minimal. When children are in conflict, listening empathically to both children helps build their confidence and ability to resolve conflicts.

Another important way to prevent or ameliorate bullying is to have discussions that help children understand how they can be an ally when other children are being intimidated or left out.

Conversations that aid children's awareness

In her wonderful book, *Creating Compassionate Kids,* by Dr. Shauna Tominey offers examples of conversations with children of all ages about subjects like resolving conflicts and coping with peer pressure and social exclusion.

She emphasizes that conversations about social issues go better when mothers take an inquiring tone which helps children become curious about their own feelings and insights. As children get older, it may be hard for them to say no when an admired child suggests they do something that makes them feel uncomfortable like teasing someone or excluding them. Ultimately, regular conversations about feelings and problem situations help children to reflect on their actions and make better choices, especially after they've done something they regret.

Of course, it takes more than one conversation to help children understand what bullying is and to develop awareness of their own relationships. Tominey suggests that parents talk to children about their own childhoods and times when they experienced or witnessed bullying.

Children often refuse to talk about the negative behavior of peers because they fear rejection or retaliation, but usually during casual conversations parents can get a sense when there is underlying stress. The signs that a child is feeling victimized often show up in physical symptoms like stomach aches or problems sleeping, and when these problems occur or mothers notice that a child feels consistently unhappy, it's time for regular check-ins after school to ask about the day.

When a child feels victimized

If a child is continually nervous about going to school, mothers can start by going to a teacher or administrator to get a wider perspective on what's happening socially. As we will see in more than one story at the end of this chapter, school refusal can be complicated. But hearing a teacher or administrator's insights can aid the process of getting children the support they need or help a parent decide if a particular environment is working for the child.

Parents need information about how their child functions socially in settings outside the home, as well as insights into the other children involved in their lives. Conferring with caring adults in a child's life helps parents learn to assimilate feedback about their child, not always an easy process.

This kind of communication with relevant adults is also an important part of advocating for them. This is especially crucial when a parent suspects there is lack of understanding about a child's special circumstances including learning or developmental difficulties, gender identity concerns, or problems with racial bias. It is well documented today that mothers of active black and brown boys often have to fight against their children being labeled as bullies and expelled from schools and daycare. This is sometimes referred to as the "school to prison pipeline."

Sometimes, schools are not responsive to parents' concerns, Administrators may deny bullying or overt racism. Mothers need to feel empowered and believe in their own abilities to help their children socially and to broaden community awareness. They need to track in-person and online that may be unsafe. When children have access to social media, online bullying is a whole new arena of concern.

The prevalence of cyberbullying

The Emmy award-winning film, *Adolescence,* a 2025 Netflix limited series, tells the four-part story a thirteen-year-old boy arrested for killing one of his classmates. As the story unfolds, viewers become aware that the boy's parents have been completely oblivious to the hours he was spending on his computer every night and the fact that he was the victim of cyberbullying, a painful situation that led him to commit homicide. In the last scene, viewers follow the boy's bereft father into the child's empty bedroom, as the camera pans the elaborate computer set-up the parents have given him, presumably to promote his academic success, but which led to a tragic conclusion. We are all learners when it comes to online threats and local law enforcement agencies are often good sources of information about children's computer use.

There are many articles about preventing bullying online, and it's interesting that parents are cautioned to look for the same signs that would indicate other types of unhealthy interaction: changes in a child's mood, hesitation about engaging with others online, sleep disturbances or changes in appetite. Then there are the problems of the children who intimidate others online. Children who engage in cyberbullying lack empathy for others, and studies have shown that empathy training can reduce online bullying. In conclusion, we might surmise that in the big picture nurturing children's empathic abilities is a key to helping them at every stage to develop healthy, fulfilling relationships.

Here are some strategies that can help children learn social skills and avoid negative interactions:

- Make rules at home that include no hurting physically or verbally through put-downs or teasing and stick to them.
- Praise children who are trying to work out conflicts on their own and support them in the process.
- Role model positive social interactions and ways of handling conflict.
- Discuss social situations on TV and point out ways people are cooperating or working out conflicts.
- When young children get into physical conflicts, help them stop and take turns expressing their feelings in words. Give them words for feelings rather than saying, "Use your words."
- Encourage children to make amends. Young children can dictate a note or do something kind for a sibling or friend.
- Listen to children's upsets and validate their emotions.

- Organize play dates and help young children share materials by taking turns. Praise children for patience when they are able to wait their turn.
- Role play at home to help a child practice speaking up with children in other settings.
- Coach an active, impulsive child to self-calm through breathing and taking a quiet time.
- Give positive recognition to an impulsive child who expresses feelings rather than fighting.
- Preview social situations like parties by talking about what will be expected and ways children can extricate themselves if they feel overwhelmed.
- Avoid labeling your child or their peers as being aggressive, mean, or uncaring. Talk to your child about ways to understand other children's motivations.
- Challenge other parents who label children who need extra support to learn social skills.
- Teach children to avoid other children who make them feel unsafe or uncomfortable and urge them to go to adults for help.
- Build community with other parents who want to raise kind, compassionate children.
- Advocate for more social-emotional learning in schools, especially empathy training.
- Expand a child's friendship pool through extra-curricular activities where they can meet children who don't attend their school.
- Engage with other parents to be sure that adults are always present when your child is involved in an activity at their home.
- Monitor online activity closely.

Mothers can be bridge-builders and network-creators. They are often change-agents in our society, and by holding the big picture that their children can learn to relate to others compassionately they help their children and all children to bring their full gifts to the world.

When mothers teach children to understand and tolerate racial and ethnic diversity, neuro-diversity, learning differences, individuality in sexual identity, and disabilities, they help children become potential allies for people who aren't like them, and in doing so they create stepping-stones to a new, less divisive world.

In the meantime, we benefit from real-life stories of how mothers manage to bring about transformation even when their lives are full of challenges.

Reflective questions:

How can parents work together to prevent their children from bullying and excluding one another?

What could the role of society be in giving status to those who treat each other kindly?

Resources:

Allen, Jessica Joelle, *The Danish Way of Parenting: What the Happiest People in the World Know about Raising Confident, Capable Kids, Penguin, 2016.*

Allison, Scott T., "Why Mothers Are Our Number One Heroes,", PhD, Psychology Today, 2013.

Barth, Diane, LCSW, "6 Smarter Ways to Deal with a Bully,", posted May 20, 2024.

Belkin, Lisa, "Why Mothers and Fathers Play Differently," New York Times, 2010.

California Department of Education, *Creating Equitable Early Learning Environments for Young Boys of Color,* Sacramento, 2022.

Cooper, Scott, *Sticks and Stones: 7 Ways Your Child Can Deal with Teasing, Conflict, and Other Hard Times,* Random House-Times Books, New York, 2000.

Freedman, Judy, MSW, LCSW, *Easing the Teasing,* McGraw-Hill, Contemporary Books, 2002.

Hyson, Marilou, Taylor, Jackie L.," Caring about Caring: What Adults Can Do to Promote Young Children's Prosocial Skills," Research in Review, Young Children, July 2011.

Lang, Li- Jun, PhD, "The Efficacy of Emotional Intelligence Training for the Emotion Regulation of Bullying Students: A Randomized Controlled Trial", NeuroQuantology, February 2018.

Mah, Ronald, *Getting Beyond Bullying and Exclusion; Empowering Children in Inclusive Classrooms,* Skyhorse publishing, 2013.

Rodkin, Phillip. Hanish, Laura, Espelage, Dorothy, *A Relational Framework for Understanding Bullying, Developmental Antecedents and Outcomes,* University of Illinois,2014.

Simmons, Rachel, *Odd Girl Out; The Hidden Culture of Aggression in Girls,* Harcourt, 2002.

Tominey, Shauna, PhD, *Compassionate Conversations,* Shambhala, 2020.

Zych, Izabela, et.al, "Are Children Involved in Cyberbullying Low on Empathy? A Systematic Review and Meta-Analysis on Empathy Versus Different Bullying Roles," Science Direct, March-April, 2019.

Here are the stories:

In the first story, when a third-grade girl complains that girls in her class are excluding her, her mother encourages her daughter to share her feelings with her classmates. In addition, she finds activities that empower her daughter and expand her friend group.

The second story reveals how a mom is able to anticipate social issues related to cliques and popularity that her daughter might have with other girls in middle school. Since her daughter has high-functioning autism, she finds an inclusive environment where she can be mainstreamed, and consequently her daughter is able to make many friends.

The third story describes a mom's journey discovering two separate situations in her son's life that involve stressful clashes with bullies. Her conversations with him energize her to move him to another school where he flourishes socially.

In the fourth story, an older sister reports that her brother has been beaten up at school and called the N-word. These incidents remind her mom of the times she was bullied as a child. Her story evolves into trying to get a whole school community to learn about diversity and inclusion.

Best Thing: Encourage Children to Express Their Feelings

Taylor Swift

Beatrice's lovely eight-year-old daughter, Lila, is a great reader and loves imagination and books. She is also quiet and reserved and has complained to her mom about others leaving her out. However, rather than suggesting ways that Lila could change her personality to gain the approval of other girls, Beatrice has urged her daughter to feel comfortable being herself. She knows that in the big picture, it will matter more what Lila thinks about herself than what others think of her.

Beatrice and her husband, Daniel, have two children. Lila is in third grade, and Emily is in kindergarten, and both attend a private school where positive values are emphasized. Lila has always been an introvert who needs time alone. Beatrice says, "Lila is a great observer. She is a deep thinker, a reader. She has a wonderful vocabulary and such a beautiful imagination that she can lose herself in her fantasies."

Beatrice and her husband are careful not to refer to Lila as shy, which would be a negative label, affecting her mindset about her ability to make friends. They prefer to say, "You're feeling shy in a situation, but you can talk to the other girls about your feelings."

Pairing up as a form of exclusion

Lila started having sensitive feelings of being left out when she was in second grade. In first grade, everyone had played together more interchangeably, but in second grade, her friends were changing, and they tended to pair up, which often made Lila feel left out. In Ronald Mah's book on bullying mentioned earlier, he points out that girls' bullying tends to be relational rather than physical.

Girls' tendencies to form pairs so they can have intimacy often leave others out. Sometimes, excluding others, giving girls a sense of power and bolsters their self-esteem. Adults can try to prevent exclusion by talking to girls about how it hurts to feel left out and encouraging them to be more empathic and inclusive.

Lila's second-grade teacher offered her a great tool for processing her feelings: she gave her a journal. Lila started writing in her journal every day, and she became more articulate about expressing her emotions and being able to express them to others. Her teachers also coached her to say things like, "I feel sad when you say I can't play" or "I have an idea for a game I want to tell you about."

Beatrice also praised Lila for speaking out about things and for developing her own voice. For a child who is quiet, talking about their feelings to those outside the safe world of home is an accomplishment that deserves recognition.

In third grade, Lila experienced some new forms of exclusion. When Lila had some disturbing instances of approaching other girls on the playground and having them go off to do something else, she talked to her teachers. They were very compassionate and validated her feelings that not feeling included was hurtful. One of the school values is inclusion, and there is a rule that children can't tell another student that they can't participate in a game. However, turning away from someone who wants to chat has a more nuanced quality to it.

Her teachers encouraged her to speak up and have confidence in her words. They organized a meeting of girls, where they talked about the pain of feeling excluded, and Lila bravely shared her experiences of being left out. The teachers reminded the group that they had all had similar experiences in their lives and that it was important to empathize with others and help them feel included. The girls were touched, and some of them wrote letters of apology to Lila. Her willingness to share her feelings changed the attitudes of some of her peers.

Coaching to express feelings

Beatrice has always explored relationships with Lila by asking her gentle questions about what she thinks. What activities with others make her happy? She often talks to her about options, pointing out what the choices might be in troubling situations, "You could try talking to the person about your feelings or find something else to do?" Which do you think would work better?" She wants to develop

Lila's judgment and confidence in her own intuitive knowing, which are her best assets in the long run.

Beatrice actively celebrates Lila for the unique person she is, even as she grows and changes with age. She's aware that it's easy for girls in our culture to become people pleasers in order to win acceptance. Beatrice and her husband, Daniel, are both teachers and have concentrated on helping Lila to be aware of her own wonderful qualities rather than on the superficial traits her peers might value.

As teachers, they know that developing their children's feelings of self-worth is the foundation for their confidence in the big picture of their growth as they go out into the world. It's important to differentiate between learning social skills and trying to change who we are to be more acceptable and lovable.

At Lila's age, she is developing the ability to understand other people's perspectives and to handle abstract ideas – like identity or intimacy.

Widening a friendship pool

Lila's parents wanted to widen her potential friendship pool, and Daniel started coaching a girls' soccer team. Lila thrived and made new friends whom she started seeing for play dates in addition to her classmates at school. Beatrice also signed them both up for *"Girls Who Run,"* an organization for girls and others who like to do long-distance running together. Again, this activity widened Lila's friendship and gave her an interest in talking to others about it. Recently, Lila and Beatrice ran their first 5K run together.

In the big picture, Lila's world has broadened so that she isn't just focused on relationships in her class at school but potential friendships with people in the outside community. She has also expanded her self-concept from being a reserved, bookish girl to one who is physically strong, can score points, run five miles, and get certificates. She has become a more interesting person to herself and to others while still preserving the integrity of her inborn temperament. In the big picture, when people accept us for who we are, we have the feeling of being seen and loved and can learn to love ourselves.

Teaching girls they don't have to please

Beatrice herself has grown in impressive ways. She grew up in Brazil, raised by her grandmother, who was loving but strict. There was no emphasis on emotions or psychology, so that's an area of learning Beatrice has had to explore on her own. She says her grandmother's love language was "feeding and taking care of me. Since my mother wasn't around, I wanted to please her. If I didn't have her approval, I was afraid I wouldn't have anyone to take care of me."

Learning to support her daughter's social skill in a culture so different than the one where she grew up has been a growth experience for Beatrice. She has worked on developing her own self-worth and finds she is especially helped by the work of Louise Hay. She uses Hay's affirmations to start the day and reads them to her daughters before they go to school, "I am safe. "I am worthy of having friends."

Reflective questions:

How can we avoid the tendency to encourage children to change the way they are in order to please others?

What are concrete ways of helping children learn to express their feelings to their peers?

Resources:

Hay, Louisa, Self-*Esteem-Motivational Affirmations for Building Confidence and Recognizing Self-Worth,* Hay House, 1990.

Hay, Louisa, *Heart Thoughts,* Hay House, 1992.

Osler, Audrey, PhD, Vincent, Kerry, *Girls and Exclusion; Rethinking the Agenda,* Routledge, 2003.

Best Thing: Find the Right Peer Group

"I understand as well as anybody the pressures of modern life, but these days of your children's lives are irreplaceable. As far as possible, try not to miss one of them."

Rob Parson

"Will my daughter be able to make friends in middle school?" This is one of the questions Naomi was asking herself as her twelve-year-old daughter, Bella, graduates from elementary school and transfers to sixth grade. Naomi is not alone in her concerns. Research at Arizona State University found that mothers of middle school children between 12 and 14 years old were more stressed than mothers of infants. The early teen years are a time when girls become more concerned with how their peers view them, and they can become obsessed with questions of popularity. Although not all girls yearn to be in the in-group, Naomi knows that Bella, like any other middle schooler, will have to learn to navigate a larger, more complex social world.

Supporting girls' friendships

Yet, in some ways, Bella isn't like every middle school girl: she is neuro-divergent, and because of that, Naomi has learned to be more equipped to support her daughter with social issues than many other parents. Naomi has been intensely involved in coaching Bella's relationships since she was two years old and diagnosed with autism. People who meet Bella now at the age of twelve, at one of her Girl Scout activities, or at a concert, may not notice that she is any different from the other exuberant and talkative twelve-year-olds. Indeed, girls are far less likely to be diagnosed with autism than boys, as their signs of being on the spectrum are often more subtle. In fact, Naomi might not have had Bella assessed if it weren't for the watchful eye of her great-uncle, who was also Bella's pediatrician.

At 22, Naomi was a graduate student in psychology when she and her husband, John, learned that she had been gifted with a surprise pregnancy. Her whole close-knit Jewish family was thrilled about the baby, and they immersed themselves in Bella from the moment she was born. Naomi felt so close to her uncle that he came to the hospital immediately after Bella was born, and Naomi kept his number on speed dial on her phone to ask him questions.

As a baby, Bella showed no times of atypical development, with her cuddly nature and early ability to talk. She was a joyful baby and toddler, and Naomi, who had left her graduate psychology program to be a mother, enjoyed being with her full-time. However, in preschool, the director noted that Bella was hitting and pushing her classmates when she couldn't get what she wanted.

Naomi tried to tell herself that these behaviors weren't unusual at that age. She would call her uncle sometimes on her cell phone from the park where Bella was having an altercation to reassure herself that everything was okay. Her Jewish uncle was gentle but said he had noticed a couple of subtle cues and wanted Naomi to check them out.

He referred her to a developmental pediatrician, who miraculously saw Bella immediately. Naomi remembers crying hysterically when the doctor diagnosed Bella with autism. But she still remembers the wise words of the pediatrician, "She's still the same delightful, intelligent child she was before the assessment." Naomi felt emotionally overwhelmed by the diagnosis, while her husband, John, seemed just to take it in stride.

Actively supporting social skills

Naomi threw herself into supporting her daughter in every way possible. When the preschool Bella attended said they needed an aide to manage her behavior, Naomi started accompanying her daughter to school daily. She also accessed a whole support system and learned how to help her daughter with pragmatic speech and the ability to relate successfully verbally and non-verbally with others. Naomi found a compassionate private elementary school for Bella, where she could mingle with more typically developing peers with the help of a hired aide. Meanwhile, Naomi finished her graduate work and became a licensed marriage and family counselor and gave birth to Dahlia, a little sister for Bella.

In her mom role, Naomi has continued to talk regularly with Bella about her relationships at school and with girl scouts. As a twelve-year-old, she is often outgoing and joyful but prone to outbursts and wanting things in her own way. Naomi has become adept at coaching Bella to calm herself when she's dysregulated and to talk about her feelings. This has been their pattern since kindergarten. "Sometimes, she'll be upset and say, 'No one would play with me today. I was all alone,' and we talk about her feelings and what choices she could make in that moment."

However, looking for a middle school with Bella has brought social concerns back into sharp focus for Naomi. She remembers her own teenage experience and some of the drama with other girls. However, she also has professional experience now with teens and their relationships.

Choosing the right social environment

In the big picture, she wants Bella to be in the most supportive, possible environment so she becomes a young woman who learns to make her own choices. Several schools she applied to weren't open to students with special needs. Fortunately, she finally found a Jewish middle school that focuses on intellectual curiosity, as well as the values of kindness and service to others. The school welcomed her, and Naomi is delighted that Bella will be getting a Jewish education.

Still, she finds that no matter where the children are going for middle school, she and her friends who have typically developing daughters have fears of having their daughters judged or rejected, and pressure to be popular or be on social media. As a parent and a professional, Naomi is in a position to help other mothers feel more confident in maintaining close connections with their daughters as they enter a new stage of development.

Reflective questions:

How does holding a vision of inclusiveness enable us to create more supportive environments for all children?

Resources:

Tang, Yun, Yang, Yin, et al. "Association of Prosocial Behavior Between Mothers and Their Child with Autism Spectrum Disorder: The Mediating Role of Maternal Parenting," Journal of Autism Developmental Disorder, March 2022.

Best Thing: Pay Attention to Social Stress

"Listening is a magnetic force"

Karl A. Menninger

Bradford started making friends before he began school in a Mommy and Me class. His mom, Cynthia, became good friends with the other mothers, and the families enjoyed playdates at the park together. They were allomothers to each other and formed a supportive network. The same children continued as a close-knit group into kindergarten, and they played together at school and continued to have playdates after class.

In first grade, a little bullying started between the boys. One child might insist that his friend does something against the rules, and then the child who carried out the orders got in trouble. Their relationships started involving physical pushing and intimidation. These were the same boys who had gotten along so well when they were younger, but now their dynamics were changing, and some boys were asserting dominance.

Her husband, Roy, felt it was just part of the boys' playful interactions. His view was that rough and tumble play between boys is normal, but Bradford was disturbed by his friends being mean and trying to have power over each other. He started playing the role of mediator between the boys, using his beginning social skills to help them get along. Cynthia says, "As an only child, Bradford wasn't used to conflicts with siblings or having to set boundaries if a brother or sister got into his things. It was painful for him to witness his friends being harsh with one another, and he stepped up to try to make peace between them."

Establishing a hierarchy between boys

In second grade, the dominance-play accelerated, and Bradford arrived home from school so upset every day that it would take him thirty to forty minutes to calm down. Since he and Cynthia had a close relationship, he would confide in her about trying to stop arguments between the children and how upsetting their harshness with each other was.

When mothers are attuned to their children, they see changes in their moods and self-confidence that others in their lives might miss, and Cynthia was genuinely concerned. Bradford had always had a happy temperament, and now he was unhappy much of the time. Cynthia knew her son and could observe how much stress he was going through because of the dynamics.

Finally, one day, Bradford made a startling declaration, "I don't like school," he said. "I want to be homeschooled." Cynthia was shocked, "I didn't even know he knew about homeschooling. We had always planned that our neighborhood public school would be where he would go. However, I was so worried about Bradford that I immediately talked to a friend I trusted about their experience with homeschooling."

Finding a place to heal

Cynthia and Bradford went to visit a private school that offered a hybrid program, half at school and half at home, and they fell in love with the teacher the day they observed. The class was reading the book *The Prince and the Pauper,* and the teacher invited Bradford to play the prince. It turned out, the whole school curriculum was based on literary classics, and all the students who had different learning needs were set up for success. They decided to enroll, and Bradford thrived.

Bradford made friends and enjoyed the harmony of smaller classes with lower teacher ratios. Cynthia missed her support group, the allomothers from the other school, who knew and cared about her child, so sending her son to private school was a big adjustment. But she was determined to help Bradford de-stress and feel good about himself.

The plan was for him to attend the hybrid school for a semester then have him return to public school However, when Cynthia asked him at the end of the term if he wanted to go back to their neighborhood school, he refused, and he was surprisingly articulate about his feelings. "If I am a plant and go back to my old school, the ground is dry and cracked, and my leaves are falling off. At my new school, I am watered every day, and I am blooming."

Returning to public school

Since Bradford had such strong feelings about transferring back, they let him stay at the private school. But at the end of the year, it didn't seem financially sound to pay private school tuition, so they made yet another change and put him back to public school, thinking he was ready to handle it. This transition occurred at the start of sixth grade when Bradford was entering middle school. He was considered a new kid, which made it hard for him to fit in with the cool group, though he found two nice friends.

Soon, some physical aggression started. Bradford had taken Aikido, and when one of the boys attacked him, he lifted him off the ground by his collar without hurting him. However, he was sent to the principal's office. Cynthia and her husband, Roy, felt he was within his rights to defend himself, but they were trying to let him navigate the situation.

Seventh grade was in a different, public middle school, and Bradford came home every day upset but refused to talk about the reasons why. Instead, he insisted on playing video games. Since they wanted him to have a time limit on games, this escalated into a power struggle. Finally, Cynthia saw that he was so stressed by school that she should just allow him to play so he could calm down. One day, Cynthia and Roy looked in Bradford's lunch box and saw that the food had been mutilated. He finally admitted that in PE boys had thrown his lunch around the room. Bradford had also been kicked and pushed into a locker, but he had been threatened not to tell anyone, or the other boys would get revenge.

Making the school aware of bullying

Roy wrote a letter to the school principal about the incidents and got results. The principal met with each of the boys and their parents individually and stated that their behavior was absolutely unacceptable. It turned out that the P.E. teacher had been present during the aggression but interpreted their play as harmless pranks even though some of the boys were getting hurt. When the adult in charge doesn't reinforce rules, impose consequences, or ask the victims of aggression how they feel, bullying goes unchecked.

Research shows that this type of social dominance often escalates in sixth grade.

Finally, the administration put Bradford in a different PE class. However, after these experiences of physical violence, Cynthia and Roy decided to put Bradford back in private school, where he flourished through twelfth grade. Bradford made lasting relationships that expanded in wonderful ways even into college.

Moreover, Bradford enjoyed the intellectual aspects of school and has now graduated from college and is looking forward to a gap year before studying genetics in graduate school. His story highlights the importance of parents really listening to children about their social experiences in different settings and exploring ways of meeting their unique needs.

Reflective questions:

How did Cynthia's ability to listen to her son empathically allow her to stay tuned to what was happening in his life?

Resources:

Coloroso, Barbara, *The Bully, the Bullied, and the Bystander,* William Morrow, 2024.

Pollack, William, PhD, Real *Boys: Rescuing Our Sons from the Myths of Boyhood,* Henry Holt, New York, 1998.

Best Thing: Think about Educating Your Community

"Those who say it can't be done are usually interrupted by those who are doing it."

James Baldwin

Rama and her husband, Ayan, were excited about their son Nebi starting kindergarten at the same public school as his sister, Anji attended. Both parents are doctors and commute to their jobs in different directions and were looking forward to picking their kids up at the same school every day. They had purchased a house in a suburb that reportedly had good schools, high test scores, and nice campuses. With her Indian background and his experience emigrating from Africa, they had both experienced prejudice, but didn't anticipate it in their new neighborhood, even though there were few people of color. Their son, Nebi, starting school seemed like a new step in settling into their new community.

Encountering racism

On the first day of school, Nebi was proud to have a new lunch box. However, about a week after the term began, Anji came home almost crying, telling her parents that a boy at daycare had punched Nebi in the stomach and called him the "N-word." Rama was alarmed that no one at the daycare had informed her of the incident and made an appointment to talk to the director.

At the meeting, Rama was direct and asked why she hadn't been told about Nebi getting hit and being called names. The daycare director said she hadn't heard about the incident. As they talked, Rama was disturbed that the director didn't suggest a way that they would protect Nebi in the future.

Rama and Ayan talked about what to do. In the big picture, they realized that Nebi would be one of the youngest children in kindergarten, and it would be fine for him to do another year of preschool, so they took him out of the public kindergarten and daycare and brought him back to his old preschool. There were several children in the preschool class who were delaying kindergarten for a year, and this seemed like a temporary solution to the new, puzzling circumstances in their lives. Nebi happily completed his bonus year of preschool and then returned to the public school.

Bullying a first grader

The problem started happening again and soon after he started, Anji came home upset again with a repeat of the same tale of aggression that had happened in the past. Nebi had been hit at school and called the N-word. In fact, Anji said the hitting and name-calling had occurred several times. Rama and Ayan were shocked. They were both in high-status professions helping people every day, and they couldn't imagine this happening to their child; the whole situation was bringing up feelings from their childhoods. Rama had been teased in school for her Indian background Ayan had confronted bias when he came to America, His reaction was, "They think of him as Black, and they are bullying him. He will have to act perfectly. That's what I had to do. It's the only way he will be accepted."

Rama didn't agree. She didn't want her son to have to be perfect, and she concentrated on making him feel brave and able to get help when he needed it. She told him that if anyone hurt him or called him a name to tell the teacher right away, something he hadn't been doing because of his quiet nature. Rama also validated Nebi's angry feelings of being hurt, and she role-played scenarios with him at home, so he could practice speaking up.

Since there were repeated incidents targeting her son, Rama knew this came under the category of bullying and talked to the principal. She was chagrined that aggression was occurring at her school, but she didn't suggest any plan for helping Nebi. In addition, as an administrator she was concerned about liability, so she refused to acknowledge that Nebi was being targeted. Rama was furious. Rama and Ayan had come to their new community with such high hopes, and now they were learning about some of its concrete realities, that their children were victims of prejudice. The suburb where Rama and Ayan had moved was 82 percent white, 0.4 percent Black, and 11.6 percent Asian, and the students were clearly not used to seeing people of color.

In the big picture, Rama wanted to help create positive change, so she asked the principal if the school had a diversity committee and offered to start one.

Educating children about prejudice

She realized that these were the neighborhood children that Anji and Nebi would be growing up with, and it seemed important to enlist their parents in educating their children about different races and cultures. Experts have long pointed out that when white parents have conversations with their children about racism, it reduces bias. However, this often isn't a priority for white parents because bias doesn't impact their lives. On the other hand, parents who have children with brown skin typically have consistent discussions with their children in order to protect them. In a groundbreaking study, research at Northwestern University has shown that parent discussions about racial prejudice with 8–12-year-old children resulted in a significant decrease in anti-Black bias.

 Rama thought deeply about the elements that create a harmonious community. She is careful not to talk to her children in a way that demonizes the young kids who have been acting like bullies at their school. Instead, she emphasizes that we live in a world where everyone is learning about what it's like to be good neighbors and friends. She knows that children can be afraid when someone doesn't look like them, but she is coaching her children to tell their peers that they don't want to be bullied and will tell a teacher.

In the process, Rama is educating her own children by buying them books that feature families of color and talking to them about how beautiful their hair and skin color are. She is teaching them about her Indian heritage and their father's African culture. In the big picture, hearing about their ancestors gives Anji and Nebi a fuller sense of who they are and the ability to extend their identities beyond the current situations. Since they have families abroad, they will be global citizens and will know people all over the world.

Research shows that mothers, in particular, have the power to buffer the long-term psychological effects of being victimized through warm, supportive interactions with their children. So, in the big picture, Rama's strategies of giving her children loving support in the face of challenges are helping to make the world a safer and more inclusive place for the generation to come, but it is still a work in progress.

Reflective questions:

How do we combat bias through the conversations we have with children and the books we read to them?

References:

Summer, Serena, *How Black Parents Can Fight Racism at School*, Rolling Out, January 2025

Katz, Karen, 2002, *The Colors of Us*, Square Fish.

Sparks, Louise Derman, *Guide for Selecting Anti-Bias Children's Books*, Social Justice Books, 2013.

Chapter Seven: The Big Picture of Valuing Your Child (And Yourself) in Real Time

Dr. Michele Borba

Is all of childhood meant to be a marathon?

I know a wonderful man who teaches science at a public high school. He is a great teacher who inspires his students to be curious and learn to do their very best academically. However, instead of enjoying his students' impressive accomplishments, he worries, more and more each year, about the overwhelming stress they experience as they apply to college. These fresh-faced young people are often convinced that their lives will be ruined if they aren't admitted to the top-rated college of their choice. The teacher knows that many high-status schools have tightened their requirements, but he's learned that in the big picture, it won't matter if his students attend the college they have set their sights on. What will make a difference is selecting an institution where they can pursue their interests and goals.

He and the college counselors in his district are concerned that the extreme pressure students impose on themselves may have long-term effects on their mental health. Today, there is evidence that chronic states of anxiety high schoolers experience often continue in college. My friend tries to help his students see that there are countless educational possibilities open to them. He feels that by living in a bubble of worry, they are missing out on their senior year, a time they will never get back. Most importantly, he wants to persuade his students to value their abilities to be lifelong learners, to be curious about the world around them, and to be able to bounce back when they don't get exactly what they want.

Unfortunately, since their first year of high school, these high schoolers have hyper-focused on building their college resumes.

Their self-esteem is based on comparison, and they worry that they are never doing enough to compete with seniors across the country. There is always the threat that someone else will get a better SAT score or write a more innovative college essay. Sadly, from a young age, these high schoolers have learned to believe their success is defined by where they stand in relation to others.

Many developmental psychologists, like Dr. David Elkind, have raised alarms for decades about the pressures we put on children. His book, *The Hurried Child,* published in 1981, has come out in two editions and become a classic. It suggests we approach the subject of young people's academic stress from a different angle, based on understanding that we are rushing children through childhood. I see the changes in childhood every day, and I'm interested in the effect of that pressure on moms who are expected to accelerate their children's cognitive abilities from infancy through college, as if they as parents are also running a race.

Why do we start children's lives with competition?

In our culture, from the time children are young, mothers are subtly encouraged to raise them to compete. As soon as a baby is born, society demands mothers to think in terms of how they can enhance their development. Historically, the months after birth are a supposed to be bonding time when mothers to get to know their babies and, hopefully with the help of allomothers, get to take care of their own physical and psychological needs for rest.

In some indigenous cultures, when people hear that a baby was born, they ask, "Who came?" This question expresses the belief that a newborn is already an individual, someone who fits into the kinship structure and is worthy of respect. The question, "Who came?" reveals humility, an acknowledgment that children are unique beings whom we need to get to know. Furthermore, asking the question "Who came?" reminds us of our inherent wisdom that a child brings a map of development that will gradually unfold.

In contrast, today, new mothers who are tuned into social media may be inundated with ideas to kick-start their child's development through stimulating activities. This pressure on mothers often revolves around an obsession with developmental norms –

considered the scorecard of what a baby or child should be doing at any given moment in time.

This viewpoint was never the intention of psychologist and pediatrician, Dr. Arnold Gesell and his colleagues when they observed thousands of children in the 1920s and 30s and created maps of the stages of development from infancy to adolescence. The Gesell Institute emphasized that children develop at their own pace and each child has their own unique timeline. However, in the latter part of the twentieth century, the idea that children's development should be accelerated began to take root, and a whole revolution aimed at making babies smarter and more physically adept at a young age began to predominate maternal consciousness.

In addition to adjusting to a whole new role, mothers were encouraged to get on board with getting their babies to develop quickly in order to equip them with a competitive edge. This preoccupation often generated chronic worry that made mothers feel they weren't doing enough to ensure their babies would have a bright future. It created the image of childhood and adolescence as a race, rather than the unfolding of a child's natural propensities.

Do milestones predict success? This idea that milestones are competitive was recently challenged by a mom who posted on a science-based parenting site, "Is there any research about whether babies who reach milestones fast do better later in life? In the study of human development, this question seems appropriate to me. Imagine a mother pressured to get her baby to walk or talk before the typical guidelines, rather than taking joy in the exciting increments of her baby's natural progress. If a mom has a child who isn't an early talker or walker, does she think less of herself and less of her child? What if her child has been diagnosed with a disability? Can she feel comfortable that her child will grow up with a sense of belonging in a culture that views childhood and adolescence as a race?

I lament mothers' worries about their children's futures because they leave out the realities of the big picture, that children flourish when people honor their timetables and support them when they need help. Throughout my career, I've observed a generation of children mature into adulthood and become active contributors to the world. The toddler who didn't walk until eighteen months became a dazzling modern dancer. The boy who didn't talk at two became an articulate investigative reporter. The child who wasn't potty trained in kindergarten has discovered his passion is aviation. I've witnessed the growth of countless children who got help for learning difficulties and found interests they were enthusiastic to pursue. The concern parents had about their children was always understandable, but in the big picture worry often robbed them of enjoying their children in real time.

If you are a new mother, dear reader, or someone planning to become one, I hope you will pause and consider the big picture that babies come with an internal map of development, and talents they are wired to express. When a person turns twenty-one, no one will care at what age they learned to talk, to be potty trained, or to read. What will matter, however, in the big picture, is how much encouragement a child receives for being curious, for pursuing their interests, and for making mistakes and sometimes failing. Please don't be misled by the corrosive idea that you can turn your child into a genius, an erroneous notion that began in the 1990s and still haunts us today. Here's how it started.

Where did the idea of baby geniuses come from?

In 1996, an entrepreneurial mom started the Baby Einstein video series. The original films showed toys and visuals interspersed with music, stories, numbers, and words spoken in seven different languages: English, French, Spanish, Japanese, German, Hebrew, and Russian. Research in the 1980s had revealed that babies have a remarkable sensitivity to learning language. The surprising question that grew out of that discovery was, "Why not teach them as many languages as possible?" That was one of the goals of the Baby Genius movement that resonated with people, and the videos that became an instant commercial success.

As it turned out, the results of genius training by video were disappointing. A 2010 study in *Psychological Science* showed that children who had viewed the videos for one month showed no more understanding of words than children who never saw them. Sound research in child development has shown again and again that babies progress in language development through reciprocal interactions with loving caregivers. Babies left alone with a TV screen don't thrive, and in fact, early exposure to screens can be detrimental.

In 1999, the American Academy of Pediatrics issued a warning about the potential negative effects of allowing children under two to engage in any screen time. The Academy reconfirmed that warning in 2011.

Why do Americans encourage over-stimulation?

The idea of turning babies into geniuses was part of an American belief system that propagated the idea that babies needed to be stimulated physically and mentally. There were innovations to enhance every area of infant development, but the effects were not always positive. Having babies watch videos of people speaking different languages didn't turn them into linguists. Putting babies in an invention called "walkers" allowed them to move around in an upright position for long periods of time, but sometimes caused their legs to overdevelop, making it difficult to walk at all. There were even cases where babies in walkers fell down stairs.

Stimulating babies cognitively with toys armed with noises and flashing lights also made it harder for babies to soothe themselves. The lack of ability to self-calm and rest was highlighted in studies that revealed that Dutch babies sleep more hours more a day than their American peers. In retrospect, baby and toddler life had become littered with apparatuses and faulty ideas that clouded people's thinking. With the growth of more and more ways to intervene in children's development, it was often difficult for mothers to find a big picture perspective.

Where can mothers turn for a nurturing, developmental approach to babies and children?

Fortunately, there was a sane voice advocating for a change in perspective about what babies and children need. That shift came from a Hungarian early childhood educator named Magda Gerber. In Hungary, Gerber studied with the famous pediatrician Emmi Pikler, who introduced new theories of infant independence and competence at an orphanage. When Gerber moved to America, she brought her prestigious knowledge of babies and children with her.

Gerber created a movement in America based on the power of simply observing and respecting babies' natural development and encouraging their independence. In 1997, she collaborated with

Allison Johnson to write a transformative book called *Your Confident Baby: How to Encourage Your Children's Natural Abilities from the Start.* Referring to the rage for accelerating babies' development, Magda said, "Childhood is not a race to see how quickly a child can read, write, and count. It's a small window of time to learn and develop the pace that is right for each individual child. Earlier is not better."

Gerber also founded an organization called Resources for Educarers or RIE in Los Angeles. The word "educarer" honors the fact that simple caring by adults provides learning for babies. For decades to this day, RIE has trained parents and caregivers to step back and pay close attention to the unique qualities of babies. The approach encourages caregivers to do less in order to foster children's independence and motivation to learn. RIE is still popular today and has been lauded over the years by child therapists for its emphasis on respecting a child's developmental timetable.

Today, actress and parenting author, Janet Lansbury, teaches RIE's respectful approach to childrearing through her books and podcasts. Her writings emphasize the wisdom of stepping back to appreciate and understand a child's development rather than intervening for quicker development. She also encourages mothers to take a sane approach as their children get older. The insight steeped in the RIE philosophy is sorely needed in a culture that pressures them to excel academically.

How can mothers assess overdoing?

Unfortunately, in a society that emphasizes competition, the mental load for mothers typically escalates as children move through the elementary grades and into middle and high school. Moms are often the coordinators of the household, the ones expected to keep track of their child's homework and tests. As students get older, its's tricky for mothers to find the balance to take care of their own needs while navigating the kind of academic and extra-curricular support they are expected to give their children. To lower their own stress, it's helpful when mothers encourage high achieving children to learn to manage their assignments independently.

However, for students who struggle, mothers are typically the ones who pick up on signs that their children feel overwhelmed by expectations at school and locate help. In 2009, a parent named Victoria Abueles made a documentary on the subject. The film is called *Race to Nowhere*, and it fully explores systemic problems of over-pressuring students in the current educational climate. It follows the lives of parents whose children are floundering in competitive learning environments, and their stories are sometimes tragic.

One mother in *Race to Nowhere* tells the horrific story of her high-achieving, musically accomplished thirteen-year-old daughter who committed suicide after receiving a failing grade on a math test. Several other children tell their own stories of feeling overwhelmed by academic pressures and trying to find ways to cope. This film is controversial and reveals contrasting opinions on what's needed to revamp our educational system and make it work for all children. But that's not the focus of this book. My concern is mothers' well-being and how they might find ways to step out of our competitive norms in ways that benefit them and their children. Everyone enjoys the times when children are joyful about their accomplishments and abilities to meet their goals. Mothers, in particular, are encouraged to take pride in their children's successes. However, when children have challenges, moms often feel bad about themselves.

Mothers in the film share honest narratives about how they gradually woke up to how overscheduled and overwhelmed their children felt in competitive learning environments. Previously, their identities as good parents were grounded in urging their children to excel. But parents in the film provide role models for re-examining our values and making changes when children feel overwhelmed, rather than going along with unworkable situations.

The film addresses competitive sports as well. As mentioned earlier, one aspect of building a college resume is engaging in athletic competition or finding impressive activities for their portfolio. However, when life feels like a race, adolescents often have the sense that their efforts are performative rather than expressive of their authentic selves.

Alfie Kohn writes,

> *"From the time we are toddlers until the day we die; we are busy struggling to outdo others. This is our posture at work and at school on the playing*

Dear reader, I want to preserve your sanity and well-being by urging you to step out of the narrow thinking of comparison and competition and give yourself permission at every stage of development to enjoy your child in real time, to cultivate a practice of mindfulness that will help you love your child and love yourself, no matter what challenges or learning difficulties they experience. No matter what their abilities, I hope you find joy in each of the increments of their growth. I urge you to help them adopt what Stanford professor, Dr. Carol Dweck, calls a growth mindset, the ability to be curious and make mistakes as part of the learning process.

You already have wisdom about what matters in life. Please take a moment and ask yourself in the big picture of your life what you have learned about real feelings of success. What variables have helped you develop a sense of purpose and fulfillment? Maintaining your own vision will enable you to appreciate your children in real-time rather than compare them with others. The key is to observe how children's interests and endeavors help them to grow in ways that they prize and encourage them to feel self-worth. They may thrive on competition or feel overwhelmed by it. We need to step out of the day-to-day pressures to assess how they are feeling. However, pay attention to your own well-being as well as theirs. Whatever their interests and abilities you shouldn't expect to control their attitudes toward learning, but you can provide a role model of self-nurturance and encourage them to pay attention to their own stress and take care of themselves.

Moms can't always convince their children that beating themselves up about the results of a baseball game or a college application won't serve them in the long run. However, a mother's ability to see the big picture of what will matter in the long run is the best foundation for staying sane and lovingly connected with their children and themselves.

Here are some strategies:

- Avoid comparing your child with their siblings or other children in conversations with others or in your own self-talk.

- Ask yourself if you are missing out on a stage of development by worrying about the future.

- Consult with professionals when you see possible delays in development.

- Notice and find joy in all the tiny increments of your child's development.

- Emphasize your child's efforts rather than just praising them when they win the game or get the A.

- Applaud your child's abilities to make mistakes and keep going.

The stories at the end of this chapter illustrate the way mothers cope with the pressures to understand and support their children in a competitive society and feel good about their own mothering.

Reflective questions:

How can we delight in children's accomplishments at every age without pressuring them to do and be more?

Why is it important not to tie our identities to our children's success in their endeavors?

Resources:

Kohn, Alfie, *Punished by Rewards,* Houghton Mifflin, 1999.

Barshay, Jill, "Proof Points: Overscheduling Kids' Lives Causes Depression and Anxiety," The Hechinger Report, February 5, 2024.

Borsato, Kate, "How to Manage Milestone Anxiety (Worrying about Your Kids Development)" Blog post, November 18, 2022.

Katie, Byron, *Loving What Is: Four Questions That Can Change Your Life,* Harmony, 2021.

Gartstein, Maria, PhD, et. al. "Exploring Temperamental Differences between the United States and the Netherlands," European Journal of Developmental Psychology, 2015.

Gerber, Magda, *Your Self-Confident Baby; How to Encourage Your Child's Natural Abilities from the Very Start,* Trade Paper, 2008.

Hansen, T. "Parenthood and Happiness: A Review of Folk Theories Versus Empirical Evidence," Social Indicators Research, May 2011.

Lansbury, Janet, 2014, *Elevating Child Care: A Guide to Respectful Parenting*, Rodale Books, 2014,

Lerner, Claire, LCSW-C, "10 Traits of Highly Sensitive Children", Psychology Today, February 21, 2022

Luthar. Suriya, "Mothering Mothers, Research in Human Development," published online, August 2015.

Luthar, Suniya, Ciciolla, Lucia, "What It Feels Like to Be a Mother: Variations by Children's Developmental Stages," American Psychological Association, 2016.

Maddox, Lucy, PhD, "How Important Are Developmental Milestones Really?" Science Focus, Clinical Psychology, 2025.

Maimona Attia, author, Vicki Abeles, Jessica Congdon, directors, *Race to Nowhere*, 2009, documentary website, *Beyond Race to Nowhere*, stream on Apple TV.

Reddy, Nancy, *The Good Mother Myth*, St. Martin's, 2025.

Taylore, Jim, PhD, "Parenting: Raise a Human Being, not a Human Doing," Psychology Today. April 19, 2010.

Wexler, Natalie, *The Knowledge Gap, The Hidden Cause of American's Broken Educational System*, Winner Silver Medal from Nautilus Book Awards in Social Sciences and Education, Avery publisher, 2019.

Wicklund, Kellie, LPC, PMN-C "When Parents Compete, Everyone Loses" Maternal Wellness Center Newsletter, October 2, 2025.

Here are the stories:

The first is from Ann La Mott's book *Tender Mercies*. She shares her chagrin about her competitiveness towards the mother of her son's best friend. Ann's son is a slow reader, and the other mom brags about her son's proficiency in reading. Her story sheds light on the big picture of comparisons and their effect on mothers' emotional well-being.

In the second story, Beatrice, a former elementary teacher, copes with having a daughter who can't adjust to school. Their daily struggles are a source of embarrassment, but Beatrice finally gets the help she needs to see her daughter's real needs and support her in effective ways.

The third story is a dramatic one from sportswriter Joan Ryan's raw portrayal in her memoir *The Water Carrier*. It details an event that propels the writer to see the beautiful qualities of her fifteen-year-old son after he is injured. Ryan honestly laments her previous attitudes toward him, which were often focused on his learning deficits. She paints a hopeful picture of transcending the limits of our problem-orientation toward children who can't measure up in our competitive society and instead views them for their fundamental value.

The fourth story underlines the reality that in the big picture we only have a finite amount of time with our children under the same roof, and life is full of decisions about how we spend it. In her son's senior year of high school, NPR anchor, Mary Louise Kelly walked a tightrope trying to balance the demands of her work with her son's needs and writes a wonderful book in the process.

Best Thing: Be Aware of Your Own Competitiveness

"Relax, we're all crazy, it's not a competition."

Anonymous

In her book *Tender Mercies*, Ann LaMott details in her extremely honest and often hilarious style, the ongoing story of her feelings of competition with another mom. The woman, whom Ann refers to jokingly as her enemy, is another parent in her son Sam's first-grade class. Ann objects to the fact that the woman wears bicycle shorts every day and looks great in them. "It feels like an act of aggression against those of us who forgot to work out after we had kids."

Feelings of insecurity at school

Ann also feels threatened because her "enemy" is highly active in the school, contributes to every bake sale, and is knowledgeable about everything that's happening. Ann castigates herself for not having figured out the more complex scheduling of first grade, namely that children get out earlier on Wednesdays. Several times, Ann has gotten there late and found Sam drawing alone with the teacher. Ann is affronted when her "enemy" approaches her on a field trip and says, "If you have any questions about the classroom, just ask me."

Prayers for Christian charity

Ann begins having so many negative thoughts about the woman that she prays for forgiveness. She feels that as a Christian, forgiveness should be easy, yet her anger at the woman increases. Finally, she writes the woman's name on a paper and puts it in her special box reserved for urgent God help. However, her ire increases as she starts to compare Sam's struggle with reading in first grade and the other woman's child who has advanced reading skills. Ann's dark thoughts continue and she says to herself,' Ted Kaczynski, the Unabomber, was also an early reader."

Feelings of intrusion

To raise the stakes, in second grade, the mother takes an interest in Sam's slower reading. She brings early reader books to Ann's house, saying her son doesn't need them anymore, and maybe Sam could read them. Ann is so incensed by the woman's intrusion that she takes the paper with the mom's name on it out of her God requests and puts an exclamation point after it.

"The enemy" keeps asking Ann for a copy of the book she authored, but Ann resists. Finally, the woman badgers her so much that Ann gives her one. After a few weeks, she runs into the woman in the supermarket who remarks, "I read your book, it's lucky your son can't read." She gives Ann a wink.

During this entire time, Ann prays ceaselessly for the capacity to forgive the woman. And everywhere she goes, she seems to run into signs touting the importance of Christian forgiveness. Moreover, a friend leaves a mysterious message on her phone saying, "God loves you too much to let you stay like this."

Liberation from comparison

Finally, one day, Ann goes to pick up her son who is playing at the woman's house. The woman invites her in and offers her tea. Ann declines. She sits inside her house waiting for her son and can't think of small talk but finally accepts the tea. At one point, she bends down to look in her son's shoes alongside the other boys to see what size the other boy wears. At that moment, Ann is at last struck by the craziness of her mental comparisons and inane competitions with her self-chosen adversary, and she feels released to be free.

This is an example of seeing in the big picture that it doesn't matter what age children learn to read. When they are adults, no one will care. It's human to notice differences, and even project what they might mean in the future, but human wisdom suggests being here and now with our children allows us to see who they are today.

Part of fully accepting children is accepting their strengths and weaknesses and realizing that our embarrassment about them comes from comparing them to others in our own minds.

Reflective questions:

How can we stay aware that children have their own journeys in learning and comparing them with others affects our well-being?

Resources:

LaMott, Ann, Operating *Instructions*, Vintage Publishers, 1993.

La Mott, Ann, *Traveling Mercies*, Anchor, 1999.

Best Thing: Get Support for Yourself

"You are braver than you believe, stronger than you seem, and smarter than you think".

A.A. Milne

It's tricky for mothers whose children can't make a successful adjustment to new situations to maintain a positive sense of self and of their parenting. As a former teacher, Ginger was excited about her daughter, Teresa, starting preschool. At three, she was very verbal and imaginative and loved seeing children at the park. When Teresa began preschool at three, Ginger tried to give her the best possible start by introducing her to her teachers before school began. The teachers were warm and welcoming, but when they started going, Teresa dissolved in tears every morning when they got there. The teachers went the extra mile and allowed Ginger to stay in the preschool class until Teresa felt safe.

After a few weeks, Ginger felt she had stayed in the class long enough. She talked to Teresa and said she was going to leave her with the teachers, and she would be back at lunchtime. However, when they got to school, Teresa's separation anxiety was so severe that she screamed and clung to Ginger as if her life was at stake at the classroom door. On subsequent days, her fears about being left at school escalated; she started crying in the car on the way, then refused to get out when they got there. Sometimes, she started crying the night before and protesting that she didn't want to go to school the next day.

Severe separation anxiety

As a former teacher, Ginger decided to take a loving but matter-of-fact approach to Teresa's fears of separation and insist that Teresa go to school. She tried to reassure her by talking enthusiastically every morning at home about how much fun she was going to have at school that day. Teresa still acted terrified, and when they got there, she refused to get out of the car. Ginger would have to lift her out of the car and bring her into the classroom. It was a painful process, and Ginger felt terrible leaving Teresaa crying and scared. It was also highly embarrassing to carry a struggling child to the classroom in front of other mothers whose children were saying goodbye without any protest. Since Ginger wasn't working outside the home, it would have been easy for her to simply keep Teresa home, but she thought preschool was such an important experience for her daughter that she didn't want to give up. However, the memories of leaving Teresa crying remained with her the whole morning.

Someone suggested that Teresa might be a highly sensitive child, and Ginger researched the characteristics on the internet. She felt Teresa had many of the factors outlined. Her skin was sensitive and she complained about the labels in her clothing irritating her. She was also hyperaware of people's facial expressions and tone of voice and had a challenging time quieting her mind to fall asleep after a busy day. Ginger found the information helpful and focused her efforts on making sure Teresa had soft clothes and story books that would calm her before sleep.

Vital help

The following year, at age five, Teresa entered transitional kindergarten, which meant a new classroom and new teachers. Since it was elementary school, Ginger was not allowed to enter the classroom to say goodbye, but she worked hard to prepare Teresa for this new step. However, Teresa continued to be upset about going to school, and Ginger still had to carry her crying to class under the critical gaze of a new group of parents and teachers. She found the mornings extremely stressful and decided that she needed help.

Ginger contacted a child therapist who specializes in unresolved problems that leave children and parents feeling bad about themselves. Ginger felt comfortable talking to her and was surprised by the big picture she offered of Teresa's issues. The therapist concluded that Teresa was having such extreme upsets about going to school because she had social anxiety. She suggested a completely different way to handle her tantrums about school, designed to reduce her anxiety and approach the experience with more calm. She pointed out that in their morning power struggles, Teresa had had no control of the situation. Ginger was loving and understanding with her, but she still forced her to go to school.

A brand-new perspective

The therapist suggested that in the big picture it was Teresa's ability to manage her anxiety that mattered as she got older. She said with her highly sensitive temperament, Teresa had to feel she had choices. Ginger intuitively felt that the therapist was right, and she started seeing their situation in a completely different way. The therapist suggested that instead of insisting that Teresa go to school, she should let her decide whether she was up to going to school every day. As a former elementary school teacher, it took a lot of bravery for Ginger to try this new way of approaching Teresa's issues, but she was determined to try.

Ginger made a brand-new plan with Teresa that she hoped would be successful. Teresa liked doing her homework, and since the teachers collected it at the doorway every morning, Ginger had a strategy. She told Teresa that they could drive to school every day, deliver her homework, and then Teresa could decide if she wanted to stay at school. Ginger kept her word, and if, after turning in her homework, Teresa said she felt scared about going inside, they went back home. Ginger also softened their morning routine. She stopped talking about how much fun Teresa was going to have at school or why it was important to be on time. In fact, Ginger did little talking. She made no attempt to convince Teresa that she was going to enjoy school. Instead, she let Teresa set the mood and express whatever feelings she was having that morning, and Ginger opened her heart every day to become an empathic listener.

On the days when Teresa decided to go back home, the therapist counseled Ginger not to make going home again feel punitive or shameful. Instead, she urged Ginger to just do what she would normally do at home and leave Teresa with her own devices.

Focus on the child's needs

Ginger had to focus on being able to relax and be compassionate with herself during this whole process. She learned that the most important aspect of the situation was learning to calm her own nervous system before relating to Teresa, since Teresa was so sensitive to her tone of voice and expressions.

Today, Teresa is in first grade, and they are continuing with the same plan. Teresa may choose to stay home a couple of days a week, but more importantly, to Ginger, Teresa has also managed to make friends at school and enjoy the academics. These are encouraging new developments.

It takes bravery for Ginger to walk this sensitive path with her daughter every day in spite of what reactions she might get from others. Teachers and other parents don't necessarily understand and appreciate what she is doing when she allows Teresa to make a decision at school every day. But Ginger gains strength from trusting her own big picture knowing, and she plans on continuing with the plan and to keep working with the therapist. Ginger is immensely grateful that the approach is working and Teresa is starting to feel successful at school.

Reflective questions:

How can we as a society let go of embarrassment about our children's struggles and think creatively about how to help them?

Resources:

Aron, Elaine, PhD, *The Highly Sensitive Child: Helping Our Children Thrive When the World Overwhelms Them*, Harmony, 2002.

Best Thing: See the Beautiful Human Being beneath the Problems

"The problem is that most people spend their lives looking but not truly seeing".

Joe Navarro

For tough-minded sportswriter Joan Ryan, who had a national reputation for calling out injustice, becoming a mother, when she adopted her son Ryan in 1990, brought unfamiliar feelings of insecurity. For starters, Ryan wasn't the cuddly baby Joan imagined, and the fact that he was often irritable with feeding problems reinforced Joan's sense that she didn't know what she was doing,

Lamenting her mothering relationship

As Ryan grew older, Joan was embarrassed when he threw a tantrum at a birthday party or in the park. When she enrolled him in preschool, she sometimes got a call saying he had hit another child or wouldn't listen to the teacher. In her book, *The Water Giver,* she recounts lying awake at night feeling angry toward herself and her child "for not being more than we were."

She also contrasted her deficits in parenting with her husband Barry's way of being with their son. He found ways to delight in Ryan, loving his sense of humor and affection for others, and the way he would say, "I love you" whenever he said good-bye.

Joan's way of coping with Ryan's struggles at school was to utilize her journalistic skills, contacting experts, arranging assessments, and analyzing reports to help him be more successful. "I seemed to believe that I could, with enough research and hard work, construct the child I wanted him to be. I became, over the years, less his loving mother and more his relentless reformer."

Enjoying intimacy outside the scrutiny of others

At home, away from anxiety about the judgment of others, there were many tender loving moments between mother and son, and Joan loved listening to his beautiful, often spiritual perspectives on the world. When he was four, Ryan wondered aloud if "maybe only God is real, and we are a dream." Ryan told Joan that he thought each person had countless boxes inside them, and at the center of all the boxes lies perfection.

However, when it came to school, there were constant challenges and assessments. In one of these evaluations, Ryan was diagnosed with a sensory processing disorder, a neurological condition that affects how the brain takes in information from various senses. This was helpful information, and Joan and her husband made many adjustments to help make his life easier, but there was always a feeling that everything about learning was a struggle, and Joan felt every tiny success was hard-won.

Seeing the preciousness of her child

When her son Ryan was fifteen, Joan experienced a lifequake that altered her perspective as a mother forever. Ryan went out on a skateboard without a helmet and fell, causing a traumatic brain injury. It wasn't clear if he would live. As Joan rushed to the ER, she realized that Ryan, far from being a problem to be solved, was the most precious person in the world to her. She found herself thinking a thought unusual to her, "God bless Ryan."

He had to stay in the hospital, and Joan left her job completely. Over ninety-four days, she shadowed her son through surgery after surgery, and frightening procedure after procedure, never knowing what the next moment would bring. As people heard of Ryan's precarious situation, they started flooding them with offers to help, with companionship at the hospital and with prayers. Joan took notes as she monitored every change in Ryan's brain, and after days and weeks of uncertainty, she began to notice a change in her own mind. "Barry and I found ourselves standing in awe of our child."

Feeling gratitude for every success

Before the accident, her focus was often on what Ryan wasn't able to do, and now every minuscule bit of progress made her want to cry. Later, she would say of this period that she developed compassion, not just for Ryan, but for the other parents she met whose children had catastrophic injuries, and for all parents who, at heart, are vulnerable because they aren't in control of everything that happens to their child.

Joan's overwhelming feeling was that she wasn't alone:

"The lucky Fatima rosary beads, the prayers … the candles lit in churches we had never seen the energy from people we had never met, the love from our family and friends – do they have the power we always want to believe they have? I looked at how far Ryan had come in a month and couldn't help but think we weren't fighting this battle alone."

Joan's book, *The Water Carrier,* chronicles the loving minute-by-minute collaboration of doctors, other parents whose children were hospitalized, friends, physical therapists, aides at the hospital, people in their town, and around the country, in rooting and praying for Ryan's slow recovery. Over the next years, Joan wrote countless news stories but always credited that time with Ryan for making her a more compassionate person.

Reflective questions:

How can mothers avoid self-blame when relationships with children aren't as close as they want, and concentrate on loving them and themselves?

Resources:

Odum- Mouton Suzanne, PhD, Golomb Goldfinger, Ruth, LCP, *Helping Your Child with Sensory Regulation,* New Harbinger, 2021.

Ryan, Joan, *The Water Giver,* Joan Ryan, Simon Shuster, 2009.

Best Thing: Meditate on Parenting Time

*"Time is relative; its only worth depends on what
we do as it is passing."*

Albert Einstein

Mary Louise Kelly was acutely aware that her son, James, was in his last year of high school, and she had missed most of his soccer games for several years. She has written an article and wonderful book called, *It Goes So Fast: The Year of No Do-overs* about her meditation on time and how fast parenting goes. Soccer was James' all-time favorite thing, and he really loved having her see him play in real time. Mary Louise would have loved to attend every minute of every game to watch her son play. Her problem: as the anchor of NPR's *All Things Considered*, she is on the air daily at 4 p.m., the same time James' games started. Her book describes getting to the point when she feels she won't have any do-overs. James's senior year is her last chance, but there are only so many times she can miss work. To add to the intensity, her son, Alexander, is playing on the same team this year.

The mental load of scheduling

Few people in our society have more pushes and pulls when it comes to time than mothers, and the process doesn't feel neutral. Mothers' anguish over the use of their time. They worry about missing out on their children's lives and missing out on their own. Part of a mother's mental load is the inordinate energy she has to devote to keeping track of time. Mothers are also usually the keepers of children's schedules, making sure that they get to school on time, show up at medical appointments, and get the form turned in for soccer by the deadline. Scheduling children's lives takes a lot of brain space in a mother's mental load.

Then there's the more profound way that mothers typically relate to time. There is the perception that whatever way they spend time, isn't the right one. There is guilt about feeling overwhelmed from being with children all day and anxiety about being away from them too much. Our perceptions can take radically different perspectives in different situations: "I'm overwhelmed and exhausted from being with a two-year-old all day, I have no time for myself," or "I feel so bad that I'm away from my child so much. I feel like I'm missing milestones, and there will never be another chance. Every moment seems precious."

The balance sheet of a mother's time

Then there is the big picture overview of time, when mothers create a kind of internal balance sheet that has to do with being the best mother that one can be within the life circumstances. That was Mary Louise's approach to her son's soccer games. For years, she apologized to James when she had to miss almost every one of them. Her son seemed mostly okay with this. His dad attended every game he could; the other parents cheered James on, and he gave Mary Louise a play-by-play outline of the game at dinner. She consoled herself that she was with him at other times during the day, and there would always be another game. However, she knew her seeing him in live action on the field mattered to him, and that was always in her awareness on some level.

The finish line

The years slipped by. There was 9th grade, then 10th, then 11th, then suddenly James was in his senior year of high school. Mary Louise was out of next times. Then she realized that, in the big picture, what people always said about childhood being over quickly was true: "The tug is just as strong when your baby is seventeen as when he's seven weeks or seven months. For me, it is in fact stronger. You blink, and the finish line is in sight. Young parents listen to me; it goes so fast."

Mary Louise says most of the working mothers she knows have made a pact with themselves. When the job and the kids collide at a given time, the kids come first. However, Mary Louse could only miss her anchoring chair at 4 p.m. on weekdays so many times. She notes that these are the dilemmas that haunt you. They aren't emergencies that demand your attention. They are the choices of how to be in two different places, and which to choose when.

The trade-off

Mary Louise didn't want to give up her job as a news anchor, but in the last year of high school soccer games, she made a tradeoff. She took six weeks off to write a book and synchronized the time with her sons' games. Some of those games would always stand out in her memory like the one when her son Alexander scored his first varsity goal, and both boys were on the field at the same time, signaling to each other that the game would go okay.

Kindness towards ourselves and our children

Then, going to the games started to interfere with her deadlines. She was behind, and she had to catch up. She had to miss some games, and in one of those, James scored the goal of his school career and clinched the league's trophy. Mary Louise felt joy for him and anger at herself. This is the moment when we benefit from seeing that in the big picture, we are trying and failing and trying again and doing our best. But in that overview, we have to include love for ourselves because in the whole trajectory we have of time available to us on earth, we also have needs, goals, careers, and relationships. Those also count in the big picture.

Reflective questions:

How has Mary Louise served all mothers by painting a non-judgmental picture of the competing demands in a woman's life?

Resources:

Kelly, Marie Lousie, *It Goes. So. Fast: The Year of No Do-overs*, by Henry Holt, 2023.

Chapter Eight: The Big Picture of Women's Health and How We Tell Our Stories

Sylvester McNutt

In 2022, tennis superstar Serena Williams revealed her harrowing fight for her life after childbirth in an essay in *Elle Magazine*. The article galvanized attention on the health risks for Black women in the US, who are three times more likely to die in childbirth than their white counterparts. Like countless courageous women today, Serena defines herself as the steward of her own physical and mental health, someone who can rely on her intuitive and informed knowing as a basis for collaborating with medical professionals. There has never been a time in history when women's stories about their own health can so readily become part of the public forum and play such an instrumental role in helping others.

Women's narratives can literally be life savers. Females are underrepresented in medical research, and women's willingness to speak out often calls attention to areas where people lack knowledge, such as an awareness of Black women's maternal health. Maternal mortality rose dramatically between 2018 and 2022, even as some researchers studying the subject had their funding rescinded. Williams framed her story to encourage all women to learn about their health issues and advocate for themselves.

The power of women's self-knowledge

In 2017, when Serena checked into the hospital to have her baby, she hoped for a vaginal birth but had to have an emergency C-section. After the surgery, she intuited that she might have a blood clot and asked the nurse for the blood thinner, Heparin. The nurse dismissed her concern, thinking the medication might affect her Caesarian wound. In that moment, Serena was convinced she was going to lose consciousness and die. In this vulnerable state, she had to fight to be heard and get the treatment she needed to stay alive. It turned out Serena was right: she did have an embolism and was rushed into surgery and given Heparin. A week later, after two surgeries, she returned home with her husband, Alexis O'Hanian, and her new baby, Olympia. She thanked her doctors for saving her life.

In another, more patriarchal era, Serena's husband or her doctor might have been the ones defining her story and deciding if it should be shared. Historically, women's stories have mostly gone unrecorded, and discussions of their emotional and physical struggles, especially losses, have been considered taboo. Williams represents the new reality where women claim the agency to talk about subjects that were formerly silenced and tell their stories in a way that has meaning for them and the potential to help others.

Silence and Women's Bodies

The censorship of stories about pregnancy, miscarriage, and birth has historically been connected to the belief that women's bodies are shameful. Before the twentieth century, the subjects of mental health and reproduction were often murkily intertwined. In ancient Greece, Hippocrates and Plato spoke of "hystera" or the womb, which they believed wandered around the body, as a cause of physical and mental distress. For centuries, on the basis of those early references to the uterus, doctors diagnosed women with "hysteria," an alleged mental health condition that encapsulated an entire range of female emotions and states of being. Women's only venue to discuss problems related to their health was in hushed dialogue with other women. Yet sometimes brave women found ways to express their stories through the arts.

The influence of the arts on medical consciousness

In 1892, a woman named Francis Ford Gilman protested a nineteenth-century medical practice that hurt women in a powerful short story called, *The Yellow Wallpaper.* In the 1850s, an American neurologist, Dr. Silas Weir Mitchell, developed a special interest in hysteria in women and proposed a rest cure as a treatment for the condition. Francis consulted him about post-partum depression after the birth of her first child. Mitchell prescribed a strict rest cure, dictating that she stay in bed with no access to reading or writing in a journal.

Although her autobiographical story, *The Yellow Wallpaper,* was fictionalized, the character, who becomes mentally imbalanced from staring at the wallpaper, reveals the oppressiveness of the practice. The story, published in *New England Magazine,* was considered highly controversial since a woman dared to critique medical practice. It was not until the 1970s that Gilman's story was recognized as an important addition to the feminist literary canon.

The painting that informed doctors about women's pain

Other women have used art to convey painful experiences that have no other vehicle for expression in polite society. In 1932, Mexican artist Frida Kahlo dared to fully depict her miscarriage through a surrealistic, medically informed painting called *Henry Ford Hospital.* At the age of twenty-four, Frida, who was living in Detroit with her husband, muralist Diego Rivera, became pregnant and miscarried after three and a half months. She asked the medical staff for accurate pictures of what her fetus would look like and proceeded to detail images of herself and her child artistically.

 Her painting reveals her body lying naked on a hospital bed, surrounded by medical instruments, with her male fetus floating above her head. A tear on her cheek reveals her sadness. The painting contrasts the personal pain of the experience with the coldness of medical treatment. Frida's artistic rendering challenges many taboos simultaneously. It asserts the right of women to tell their stories in all their complexities. It also stretches traditional ideas about the definition of what it means to be a mother. In Frida's eyes, carrying her fetus for three months validates her experience of motherhood and the pain of maternal loss.

Her painting continues to educate the medical community today. In 2015, Dr. Fernando Antelo published an article in the *American Medical Association Journal of Ethics* called "Pain and the Paintbrush: The Life and Art of Frida Kahlo." Dr. Antelo says, "Kahlo's paintings serve as a medium to visualize pain and its impact on the human condition. We witness the suffering, grief, and doubt in Kahlo's paintings: through them, we can contemplate the experience of pain from the perspective of the patient."

Like Francis Ford Gilman's story about a forced rest cure, Kahlo's painting offers an authentic expression of personal experience that defies the norms of the day.

Fiction as a window to mental health

By the 1960s, some attitudes towards women's self-disclosure had become less restrictive, but there was still no venue for women to speak publicly about issues from their own lives. In 1966, poet and novelist Sylvia Plath expressed her experiences in a mental institution through a semi-autobiographical novel called *The Bell Jar.* The book, released under the pseudonym Victoria Lucas, offers a graphic and occasionally humorous portrayal of depression, anxiety, and mental breakdown. The novel's protagonist, Esther Green, a college student, finds societal expectations for women to be suffocating, like being inside a jar, and she is institutionalized temporarily, as was Plath in real life.

The novel reveals the state of the entire field of mental health in the mid-twentieth century. Although Sylvia committed suicide after its publication, the novel broke barriers by normalizing discussions about mental illness and the effects of conflicting societal pressures on women.

Revelatory memoirs – a new age of honesty and advocacy

The seventies ushered in some first-person accounts about women's health. One of the most widely influential memoirs on the subject was *Our Bodies Ourselves*, published in 1970 by the *Boston Women's Health Collective*. It, aimed at advancing more open public discourse about women's health and empowering women to learn about their own bodies.

The 90s and 2000s evolved into a time of women's memoir abundance, honest narratives by women from every cultural and economic group. Many of them are pivotal works that reshape public understanding of critical health issues. Their existence chronicles women's courageous fight to speak honestly about events in their own lives.

Here are a few of the many titles that have brought inclusive voices and provocative subjects into the conversation and educated the public on health issues that have been historically hidden.

Depression - 1998

In the 1998 memoir, *Willow Weep for Me, A Black Woman's Journey through Depression,* Meri Nana- Ama Danquah chronicles her depression, beginning in 1992 Los Angeles, when the verdict in the Rodney King trial caused LA to spiral into rioting. As a Ghanian-American woman, reaching out for mental health treatment is considered a weakness. Danquah explores the intersections of depression with domestic abuse, systemic racism, immigration, pregnancy, and single motherhood. In 2015, she was chosen as the spokesperson for the National Mental Health Association for a campaign on clinical depression targeting African American women.

Loss of a child -2005

In *Beyond Tears Living After Losing a Child,* nine women share the circumstances and grief of losing a child with honesty and compassion for one another. It also includes the voices of children whose siblings died, adding to our knowledge of how to help children with grief.

Stroke - 2006

In *Tell Me Everything You Don't Remember,* Christine Hyung-Oak Lee describes having a stroke at the age of thirty-three and recording her symptoms as they took place. It is especially relevant because women are more likely to have non-traditional stroke symptoms.

Auto-immune disease - 2008

In *Two Kinds of Decay,* Sarah Manguso explores her nine years of trying to understand and treat a mysterious and rare autoimmune illness. Her book is significant because women are three times more likely to suffer from autoimmune disorders, making up 80 percent of the people who develop them.

A mom and son's dual diagnosis of ADHD - 2010

In *Buzz: A Year of Paying Attention,* Pulitzer-Prize-winning author Katherine Ellison explores the benefits of various therapies and medications, supplements, neurofeedback, and even a visit to the Dalai Lama as a support for ADHD. Her curiosity, authenticity, and love of both her own and her son's struggles with ADHD highlight the many ways mothers can bring insight and information to collaborate with medical practitioners effectively.

Health risks of living in poverty -2014

In *Hand to Mouth: Living in Bootstrap America,* Linda Turado, a mother married to an Iraq war veteran, exposes the stereotypes that middle-class people have about the poor. From her life experience, Turado, who sometimes worked three jobs at a time, strongly asserts that criticizing low-income women for making poor health choices like smoking reveals a societal perspective of privilege and callous advantage in our country.

Cancer- 2023

In *Little Earthquakes,* psychologist Sarah Mandel shares the trauma of discovering that she had stage 4 breast cancer right before she gave birth to her second baby. In her private practice, Mandel had often suggested that her patients create a narrative account of the traumas they have experienced. She decides to follow her own advice, and her story includes her feelings of shame for being a sick wife and mother, and touching examples of conversations about her illness with her girls. Right before her death, the same year her book came out, Sarah bravely posted a TikTok video of her cancer journey and loving relationship with her family.

A Voice for Disabled Parents - 2025

In *Unfit Parent: A Disabled Parent Challenges an Inaccessible World,* Jessica Slice shares her journey of coming to understand her disability and the lives of other disabled parents. *Unfit Parent* proposes the idea that moms don't have to conform to society's perfectionistic standards and can find simplified ways of meeting children's needs.

The avalanche of digital storytelling

Groundbreaking stories about health have not just come out in books. Women began posting and blogging about their lives after the launch of YouTube in 2005. While more effort has to be made to get more low-income women access to the internet, being able to post online has generally been an equalizer.

Whether personal narratives about health are in the form of a book, an Instagram post, a tweet, or a magazine essay, they allow readers to hear from those living with different health conditions and learn from them.

The big picture of countless women sharing, in so many ways, is one of diversity but also commonality and mutual concern. We live in a world where women of every race, ethnicity, and income level experience the threat of not getting the care they need. It's important today for more low-income mothers to tell their stories so that they and their children do not remain invisible in our profit-driven society.

The need for more knowledge about women's health

In recent years, some women's health issues have become crises. There are articles and books about the effects of changing legal statutes banning abortion and the risks to women's psychological and physical health. These changes, coupled with the gutting of research on women's health issues, make this a pivotal time for people to feel empowered to learn about health issues and make good decisions.

Research shows that mothers often neglect their own health because of the demands of work and pressures to live up to the standards of intensive parenting. Stories of women informing themselves about their illnesses, listening to their own inner dialogue, and monitoring their own well-being can empower people to pay attention to health issues. These narratives also paint the big picture that all lives matter.

Dear reader, wherever you are in your journey, you are creating your own story of health. I hope you remember that you can be a warrior, a being capable of tuning into your own body, mind, and spirit and accessing the information you need to advocate for yourself when you need to and create well-being in your life.

I hope you will consider the simple yet restorative practice of journaling about your health. You can begin to value your own stories through writing about them for your personal reflection. It may lead to your sharing them with others.

The in-depth stories at the end of this chapter show the range of health issues, including loss, that impact the lives of mothers. All of these women have gained remarkable knowledge and advocated for themselves and their children in ways that would not have been possible in the past. Their journeys have allowed them to help others.

Reflective questions:

As health issues become more politicized, how can parents support each other in accessing accurate information?

Why is networking so important to combat the isolation parents feel when they or their child has health issues?

Resources:

Antelo, Fernando, MD, "Pain, and the Paintbrush; The Life and Art of Frida Kahlo, " AMA Journal of Ethics, 2013

Bueno, Julia, *The Brink of Being: Talking about Miscarriage,* Virago, 2020, Winner the British Poplar Medicine Book Award, 2021.

Balch, Bridget, "Why We Know So Little about Women's Health," AAMC News, March 26, 2024.

Brill, Stephanie, Pepper, Rachel, *The Transgender Child: A Handbook for Parents and Professionals Supporting Transgender and Non-binary Children,* Updated edition, Cleis Press, 2022.

Cohut, Maria, PhD, "The Controversy of Female Hysteria,", Medical News Today, Oct 13, 2020.

Colino, Stacey, "Women Are Still Under-Represented in Medical Research. Here's Where the Gender Gap is Most Pronounced," Time Magazine, 2024.

Danquah, Nana- Ama, *Willow Weep for Me, A Black Women's Journey through Depression,* W. W. Norton, 1998

Gilman, Frances Ford, *The Yellow Wallpaper,* Orchises Press, April 1990.

Kahlo, Frieda, *Henry Ford Hospital (Painting),* Wikipedia.

Betterhelp Editorial Team, medically reviewed by Guarnaccia, Melissa LCSW, and Ciletti. Nicki M. Ed. LPC, "Why Does Self-Care for Mothers Matter for Mental Health?" Updated August 2025.

Manguso, Sarah, *Two Kinds of Decay, A Memoir,* Farrar Straus and Giroux, May 2009.

Pennebaker, James, PhD, Smyth, Joshua, PhD, *Opening Up by Writing it Down: How Expressive Writing Improves Health and Eases Emotional Pain,* Guilford, 2016.

Perez, Caroline Criado, *Invisible Women: Data Bias in a World Designed for Men,* Abrams Press, March 12, 2021.

Plath, Sylvia, *The Bell Jar,* Heinemann, 1963.

Turado, Linda, *Hand to Mouth; The Truth about Living in Bootstrap America,* GP Putnam and Sons, *2014.*

Williams, Serena, "How Serena Williams Saved Her Own Life," Elle Magazine, April 6,

Here are the stories:

In the first story, Katie does her own research and discovers powerful spiritual and psychological tools to fortify her transformational approach to cancer. She has learned not to use the word "fight" when she refers to the disease, but instead, she talks to her cells in firm but loving ways. Her story also provides a role model for communication with an older child in honest, reassuring ways. Katie's story is so filled with vital information that she should write her own book. For now, we are lucky to have her story.

In the second story, Amy holds everything together while she cares for her dying father, but finds she needs help after unexpected miscarriages. She discovers the power of getting support for grief in a culture that doesn't acknowledge it.

The third story introduces Linda Goldman, who has become a national expert on grief and helping children handle loss. After giving birth to a stillborn baby girl named Jennifer, Linda took a life-changing grief seminar with expert Elizabeth Kubler-Ross and has written six books on grief-related subjects.

In the fourth story, Addie uses her career research skills to find out what's wrong with Lila, her bright teenage daughter, who suddenly is too exhausted to function. Others dismiss Lila's exhaustion as a form of school refusal, but Addie knows Lila loves school. Through perseverance and collaborations with multiple doctors, Addie finally finds the reasons for her daughter's malaise and gets her the treatments she needs for a complete recovery.

In the fifth story, beautiful, super-talented Guila gets her dream job but becomes so pressured that she has a mental breakdown. She and her husband view it as an aberration until it happens again after she gives birth to their first baby. Together, they make life-changing decisions about how to normalize mental health issues in their family and in the world.

In the sixth story, tennis star Naomi Osaka protects her own psychological well-being by refusing to meet with reporters after playing at the French Open, a stance that sets an example for other athletes and people in high-pressure situations.

In the seventh story, a car accident that traumatizes her four-year-old son propels Darcy into new learning and a new career.

Best Thing: Think of Yourself as Strong

"The brain and the nervous system weave into all of the tissues of the body and affect them in important ways."

Clifford N. Lazarus, PhD

Katie became an expert on cancer when her best friend, Eliza. was diagnosed with breast cancer. As a cosmetologist, Katie even created a deodorant for Eliza, which other consumers liked and purchased. Now, eight years later, her dear friend's health is still flourishing. However, during the information-gathering period, Katie had the thought, "I'm going to need all this information someday." Katie continued her interest in health, both medical and psychological, and often tuned in to "what she calls the angelic realm" for answers. Although she had left her career in cosmetology to spend full-time with her husband, Eric, and son, Nicholas, she often tried to help people with health needs and challenges.

Last year, when Katie got a rash on her breast, she intuitively knew something was wrong. After a punch biopsy, she learned that she had a very challenging form of breast cancer. Her son came into her room unexpectedly when she was crying after hearing the diagnosis and asked what the matter was. "I could see he was visibly upset, and I didn't want to dismiss his feelings, so I told him that I had just found out I have breast cancer. But I said with absolute conviction, "You have a strong mom, and I'm going to work really hard to heal this."

Keeping her son in the loop

Katie's father, Bob Royeton, who died a year earlier, was a highly regarded child therapist, and she knew that telling the truth was imperative for children because they can sense when you're not telling them something because your energy isn't aligned with your words.

She also kept Nicholas constantly aware of each procedure. She was diligent about talking to him in a calm matter-of-fact way without any fearful energy. She told him about the scans and the MRIs as she had them and described the chemotherapy and radiation she would undergo. In addition, Katie emphasized all the positive information she was gathering that would help her get better and told him to come to her anytime with questions. Equally important, her husband, Eric kept life normal, taking Nick to all his baseball games and countless other activities that were part of her son's life.

Focusing on emotional healing

Katie felt strongly that she had to include emotional healing as a foundation for restoring her health. She worked on ridding herself of the kind of negative self-talk she feels is so often embedded in women's psyches, like: "I'm not worthy, I'm not thin enough, young enough, pretty enough, good enough." She also stopped reading anything negative about her type of cancer and its prognosis.

Instead, she embarked on a multi-pronged big picture journey toward positive health, studying all the recent advances in sources like PubMed, NIH, and other journals. She also started seeing a naturopath in addition to her oncologist. Her studies convinced her to adopt a plant-based, alkaline diet, take powerful supplements, and a weekly IV of vitamin C. But most importantly, she checked in with her body several times a day about what it needed. "I concentrated on not feeling like a victim but someone who was learning and healing.'

In addition, Katie used visualization every day to protect her healthy cells during the treatment by imagining a beautiful color enveloping her body. She would also talk to the cancer cells like little children, telling them they had two choices-either revert to being normal cells or die and go back to the source.

"I was extremely motivated to do the work, and a big part of that was the way I talked to myself. I never used the word "fight" to refer to the cancer but often used the word "heal." I knew the cancer had come to me for a reason and that I had learning to do, letting go of old patterns, doing everything for everyone else, and depleting myself. That's not getting closer to God, and who is God but my true inner essence?".

Do you want to be here?

The challenging work of trying to heal on every level took enormous energy, and a couple of times Katie asked her deepest self, "Should I just give up?" Her answer was always no. "I knew I still wanted to be here, and I didn't want to be away from Nick."

At last, after almost a year of treatment, Katie was able to tell her family and friends that she was cancer-free. Nicholas responded with a huge smile and then went off to play baseball. "I'm a different person now than when I started," Katie says, "I actively love myself and I'm already experiencing the wonderful energy of being over fifty and really coming into my true self, not who others think I should be, but who I really am."

Katie let go of many negative beliefs about herself as she moved through cancer treatments.

Reflective questions:

How did Katie blend intuition and scientific knowledge in her healing journey?

What is the relationship between negative self-talk in emotional healing?

How did self-love play a strong role in Katie's healing journey?

Resources:

Lazarus, Clifford, PhD, "Can Visualization Techniques Treat Serious Diseases? The Amazing Power of the Mind-body on Psychoneuroimmunology," Psychology Today, January 26, 2016.

Best Thing: Talk to Others about Your Loss

*"Women's health is a priority in breaking barriers
and making extraordinary strides."*

Vincent Otieno

Amy works as a lobbyist for a state medical association, and she is currently writing a paper on maternal health. For the past fourteen years, medical issues have preoccupied both her professional and personal life. She married her husband, Tim, fifteen years ago and started a family. They couldn't have imagined all the challenges that would emerge as part of that process. Amy has worked hard to live her values in her personal and professional life, and they have often seemed intertwined.

Disrupted life plan for a grandpa

Growing up in a divorced home in San Francisco, Amy was exceptionally close to her father, Bruce. One of the reasons she was excited about having a baby was to have him play the role of grandfather. Her sister, Jessica, felt the same way and even adopted a little girl as a single parent while looking forward to having her dad involved in her life. Then, came devastating news: a medical test revealed that Bruce had a rare form of advanced-stage cancer and since Bruce didn't have a partner, Amy and her siblings arranged for every aspect of his care. "It truly felt like a meteor came out of the sky and took out my dad. He ate healthily, exercised, and seemed like the last person who would get cancer. While caring for my dad and spending time with him, I learned not to take anything for granted and to enjoy every moment."

Sharing women's stories

Her daughter Emily, who is now 12, was born six months after Bruce died. So, Amy's pregnancy and the first months of motherhood were interlaced with sadness that her father was missing from this huge transition in her life. She felt strongly that she wanted Emily to have a sister or brother and began trying for another child.

She became pregnant but then had a miscarriage, an event she had never imagined. Then, excited about reaching the three-month mark of another pregnancy, she miscarried again. Amy was devastated and decided to break the taboo of talking about the subject at work. In her male-dominated field, these subjects are not discussed, but in the big picture, Amy prioritized her needs and told one of her colleagues about her loss, a very compassionate woman who suggested that Amy get grief counseling. Amy's bravery in telling her story is part of the ongoing evolution of women valuing and sharing stories that they would have been deemed inappropriate in the past.

The power of grief counseling

Amy followed her guidance and found a therapist who could help her with her grief. "I don't know why I didn't think of that myself, but talking to a therapist was so supportive. I learned how heartbreaking and challenging it is for women to become mothers, and I want to respect and honor women's journeys in whatever form their motherhood takes, unless, of course, they choose not to.".

Later, Amy was ecstatic when she was able to conceive and carry her son, Benjamin, to term. "I was so grateful and overflowing with love for him. "After all that trying, being able to give birth to her son appeared like a well-earned miracle. Ben is now eight.

Amy says family is everything to her, and she maintains close ties with her sister and niece. She was also involved with her mother-in-law's medical care and getting her established in assisted living. "She was a huge support to our family when Emily was a baby, and I wanted to be there for her." Before her mother-in-law passed away, Amy took her children to see her regularly.

Amy's appreciation and love for her mom grew when she became a mother herself and fully realized how wonderful and hard it is. She remembers calling her mom while she drove to work on a Monday morning exhausted from caring for a toddler all weekend and relieved to be going to the office where it was quiet. It was amazing for Amy to realize that when she was born her mother had had three children under five. Amy reflects: "Being a mom now, I understand the depths of love you have for your children that can be hard to express. I see that same love in mom's relationships with Emily and Ben and the other grandchildren."

Creating a compassionate medical system

Amy's job has helped her learn to navigate the medical system, but her life as a loving daughter setting up care for her father and mother-in-law and getting support for herself after miscarrying means that she had to bring personal knowing into her career. Her life leads us to the question of how women's experiences and learning about motherhood can inform the workplace and the world.

Reflective questions:

How can we reframe our public consciousness to actively support people through grief experiences?

Resources:

Devine, Megan. *It's OK That You're Not OK: Meeting Grief and Loss in a Culture that Doesn't Understand*, Sounds True, 2017.

Best Thing: Learn How to Help Children with Grief

"When life issues are unexpressed or unacknowledged, they become locked in 'frozen blocks' of time."

Linda Goldman

Experiencing miscarriage can be a very isolating experience because of the cultural gag rule of delaying announcements of pregnancy to the three-month mark. Miscarriages often occur before anyone even knows a woman is pregnant. It's hard for women to reveal that they had been pregnant and have lost the baby. Mothers often feel that miscarriage means they've failed in some way, and the guilt can make it hard to share their experiences. This is doubly hard with a stillbirth when a tidal wave of grief and self-blame engulf a woman, making it hard to get support. Maternal grief is often very lonely.

Linda Goldman knows about loss from personal experience and from the hundreds of children and adults she has helped over the years to handle grief through her counseling and her prodigious writing on the subject. Linda miscarried in her first pregnancy in her fifth month, but later she and her husband, Michael, were thrilled when she was able to carry her little girl to term. However, in the ninth month, the doctor couldn't hear a heartbeat, and the baby was born still. They named her Jennifer.

Asking others about loss

Linda and Michael both felt devastated, and they called their wise friend, Jim, who came to be with them at their house. Linda worried about Jennifer. "What will happen to her? She and Michael believed Jennifer was in a heavenly realm, and Linda didn't want her to be all alone. "Who will care for her? Who will be her mother?" Then, a colleague, Olga Worrall, a nationally recognized healer who had twin boys pass away when they were a year old, told her, "You will always be Jennifer's mom." The statement was very comforting and allowed Linda to feel that Jennifer was safe and protected. Linda was forever grateful for these people who appeared in this part of her life's journey.

At the time Jennifer died, the subject of stillborn babies was taboo. Linda asked a clergyman for advice, "Do we need to have a funeral, a burial, a naming?" His immediate response was, "You don't need to worry about that. In this religion, she is not considered a life." But Linda and Michael did consider Jennifer's brief time on earth a life, and they had a service for her in their home and buried her in a cemetery. To this day, forty-three years later, Linda lights a candle on the day of Jennifer's birth and death. She still feels deeply connected to her.

Helping children with grief

A few years later, Linda and Michael were thrilled to give birth to another child, Jonathan, and he brought them tremendous amounts of joy. However, Linda was still interested in the subject of grief and loss, especially with children. When Jonathan was about three, she left him at home with Michael for a week and traveled to El Rito, New Mexico, to attend the Elizabeth Kubler-Ross," Life, Death, and Transition" workshop. It was life changing. As a former elementary school teacher, Linda felt inspired to focus on how professionals and parents can help children travel in healthy ways through the losses that occur during their childhoods. She knew from past experience that unresolved grief and loss can impact academic success.

She studied and became a licensed counselor specializing in grief and a fellow in Thanatology, the scientific study of death and the practices associated with it. In 1992, she wrote her first book on the subject: *Life and Loss, A Guide to Help Grieving Children*. Since then, the book has come out in three editions, a classic edition, and has been translated into other languages. Linda was particularly happy when it was translated into Ukrainian, because of the tremendous ongoing loss of life and property there, and because she is the granddaughter of a Ukrainian orphan who relocated to the United States many years ago.

Supporting gay youth

When Jonathan was in eleventh grade, he spent a year abroad in China. Upon his return, he announced to Linda and Michael that he was gay. Linda and Michael responded with total acceptance, and as a result, Linda wrote a book to help other parents and young people navigate their thoughts and feelings called *Coming Out, Coming In, Nurturing the Well-being and Inclusion of Gay Youth in Mainstream Culture.* Jonathan is an adult now, and a few years ago, he fell in love and got married. Down the road, he and his partner adopted twins, and now Linda is experiencing the delight of being a grandparent.

Linda's life illustrates in remarkable ways how the transition of pregnancy and birth can lead us in whole new directions if we listen to our intuition. If she hadn't given birth to baby Jennifer, her interest in grief and her ability to help so many people may never have emerged. Even after Jennifer's death, it would have made sense to return to work in elementary teaching. Yet, after attending the death and dying workshop, Linda saw that in the big picture, people need to learn how to give children help when they have grief in their lives, and as a result, she made that her mission. Her ability to open herself to new learning is part of the revolution of gaining knowledge about health in this age, through the melding of intuition and information.

Reflective questions:

Why is it important to name a baby lost through miscarriage, stillbirth, or later passing?

How do rituals help us stay connected with someone we have lost?

How can we educate teachers, clergy, and medical professionals to handle grief in sensitive ways with adults and children?

Resources:

Goldman, Linda, *Life and Loss: A guide to Help Grieving Children,* Routledge, 1994.

Goldman, Linda, *Coming Out, Coming In: Nurturing the Well-Being and Inclusion of Gay Youth in Mainstream Society,* Routledge, 2008.

Best Thing: Trust Your Observations

"Each time a woman stands up for herself, without knowing it, possibly without claiming it, she stands up for all women."

Maya Angelou

As so often happens, life prepares us for situations and events in ways we don't anticipate. Addie's dual career turned out to be a good foundation for researching her teenage daughter Lila's perplexing health issues. Initially, Addie worked as a product manager for Pfizer, which offered her an introduction to the world of scientific research. Later, she became q parent educator for an international organization called Resources for Infant Educarers, mentioned in the last chapter, a philosophical approach focusing on observing children's natural patterns of development. In addition, she earned a master's degree in human development.

Her daughter Lila's first serious illness was mononucleosis in seventh grade. She recovered, but then in high school, she came down with influenza Type A and B, as well as pneumonia, and had to make up two months of schoolwork. Consequently, she became part of the home and hospital program through the school district.

Puzzling symptoms

Lila continued to have other symptoms like dizziness and even fainted on occasion. She would get tired after any exertion. Even normal weekend activities left her feeling exhausted the next day. Addie was frustrated that their pediatrician dismissed Lila's issues as a form of school refusal. Addie knew that in the big picture, Lila was excited about learning and about school, and she trusted that understanding. In fact, Lila was in a special advanced program and looked forward to her coursework the following year. So, Addie continued her pursuit of information on adolescent health problems occurring in adolescents.

Long-term illness

When she and her husband, Don, a former consultant at Pfizer, consulted with a second pediatrician, a woman who had been in practice for decades, the doctor said she had seen Lila's condition a few times over the years. It tended to occur with tall, thin young people and lasted a long time, but she had no intervention to suggest. Addie and Don kept looking for answers to Lila's health challenges. They consulted many specialists over several years: a rheumatologist, an osteopath, an infectious disease specialist, and a naturopath for treatments. As a result, they had blood tests to assess Lila's viral load and immune system function.

Then, they finally arrived at a diagnosis of Postural Orthostatic Tachycardia Syndrome (POTS), a syndrome that causes dizziness, fatigue, and heart palpitations. But Lila persevered with her schoolwork through various programs after leaving high school. Addie comments on her challenges, "Having a chronic illness means the loss of friends. There's a lot of isolation. It was hard for Lila to see her sister and friends have lots of activities in life. But she has worked hard on her schoolwork with impressive results."

Lila has now achieved remarkable academic success. Her health issues have improved, and she has learned to manage them. She was recently accepted and even courted by colleges where she applied for next fall. Her prognosis looks good, and she is excited by plans to live in the dorm at the school she accepted.

Importance of other moms

Through her continued research, Addie has gotten to know mothers whose children have similar conditions, which is a tremendous support. Like Addie, they have all been researching their children's illnesses and making accommodations to support them. They are the new breed of moms, who feel empowered to look at the big picture of their children's health; and to keep learning so they can collaborate with medical professionals. They have all found ways to advocate for their children, and they benefit tremendously from their collaboration with each other.

Addie has put her outstanding research skills to good use diagnosing her daughter's illness. Her ability to tap outside resources has made all the difference.

Reflective questions:

What if Addie had gone with the idea that her daughter was just trying to get out of her schoolwork?

How can any mother actively pursue accurate information on health issues in our current climate?

How can mothers with similar health issues find each other and offer mutual support?

Resources:

Rosenberger, Peter, *Hope for the Caregiver; Encouraging Words to Strengthen your Spirit*, Worthy Inspired, 2015.

Best Thing: Share Mental Health Concerns Compassionately

"Taking care of your mental health is an act of self-love."

Giulia traveled from Italy to Georgetown University in Washington, DC as a freshman with a vision: she would study business, make her way in the fashion industry, marry a wonderful man, and become a great mom. She met Mark during the first few days on campus, and they began doing everything together, but Giula was still very serious about her studies and life direction. After graduating, they married and settled in San Francisco, where Guila got an exciting job in the fashion industry and Mark explored writing and a career teaching high school history. They joked that Giula was the stable, confident one, who knew what she was doing, and they were both excited about having children.

A surprising breakdown

Giula enjoyed her work and felt successful. When she was 27, she got a job at a trendy new firm, but it wasn't easy to understand what her co-workers expected from her. She started insisting that Mark read the emails she was sending and continually obsessed that her work wouldn't be good enough. Mark was shocked, "Where had the confident, competent Giula gone?" More shock followed when Giula suddenly had a mental breakdown and had to be hospitalized. After months in a psych ward, Giulia was thrilled to come home. She and Mark viewed the experience as an anomaly, something that didn't make sense in their charmed life as a couple.

Becoming a mom

Giula had always wanted to be a mother, and she and Mark were both thrilled with their son, Jonas, who was born in 2014. Giulia had wanted to be a mom from the time she was in her teens, and she and Mark reveled in every aspect of their new baby. Since Giulia was the primary breadwinner, they decided that Mark would stay home with Jonas and Giulia would return to her job after her four-month maternity leave. Then came the signs that Giulia wasn't doing well, and she had to return once more to be hospitalized. The doctors viewed Giulia's breakdown as part of post-partum depression. It was heartbreaking for Mark and Guila for her to be separated from Jonas, but he took the baby to visit every day. Jonas demonstrated his first abilities to crawl in the well-appointed psych facility.

Self-kindness about mental health

After a few months, Guila returned home and was joyful to be reunited with baby Jonas, and Mark found help in a support group. He had become the primary parent, and Giula worked hard to become a stable, loving force in her son's life again. When she imagined herself as a mom at the age of eighteen, her fantasy hadn't included having a mental health crisis. Few people have those concerns, and unfortunately, most mental health issues that mothers experience go unrecognized and untreated. But Giula worked in therapy to accept the reality that she wasn't the mom she fantasized she would be, but she was still trying to be the best version of herself that she could.

Changing the world through openness

As we all know, mental illness carries a huge stigma in our culture, but Guila and Mark made a life-changing decision to share their experiences with others. She and Mark decided to share their story to help others get help with mental health issues. So, in 2017, Mark's memoir, *My Lovely Wife in the Psych Ward,* describing Giulia's mental breakdowns in detail, was published. It has become an international bestseller. They also created a website to share their stories, and they give talks together in various venues, including schools. In choosing to go public with their story, Guila and Mark were looking at the big picture of our society and the need to break down archaic attitudes that stigmatize those with mental health issues.

Now the mother of two lively, healthy boys, Giula still gives talks, sharing her story with others. She says, "I know my mental health has to be a huge priority in my life. I have to devote myself to therapy and taking care of myself emotionally and physically. I work hard to make sure my children are validated for their big feelings and can talk to me about anything."

Reflective questions:

What is the double bind for mothers who feel that they have to present an image of perfection to the world, asking for mental health support?

Do you or people in your life benefit from mental health support?

How can we adopt a new, wider lens about mental health that benefits our children and generations to come?

Resources:

Lukash, Mark, *My Lovely Wife in the Psych Ward,* Harper Reprint, 2017.

Best Thing: Set Boundaries That Work for You

"Self-care is how you take your power back."

Lahla Delia

Naomi Osaka was born in Japan on October 16, 1997, the second girl to a Japanese mother and Haitian American father. She started playing tennis at age three. When she was four, the family moved to New York, where her father's family lived. Inspired by the way Serena Williams' father had trained her to be a tennis champion, Mr. Osaka started teaching his own two daughters in a similar style. Naomi didn't attend a structured school program because of her intense concentration on the sport, and she understood at a young age that she would become a professional as an adult. To meet those goals, the family moved to Florida when she was older, as there were more opportunities to train. When she was fifteen, she worked with tennis coach Patrick Tauma in anticipation of entering some high-stakes competitions.

But since she had been born in Japan and identified with that culture, her parents decided that she would represent Japan in the competitions. She did well and defeated former US Open champion Samantha Stosur at the Stanford Classic. Two years later, in 2018, she won the US Open, defeating Serena Williams. She was ranked number one for the first time when she won the Australian Open in 2019.

Reacting to vindictive media posts

Naomi had a huge following on social media, but later reported how stunned she was by online comments saying she didn't deserve to win. She perceived the comments as vindictive and admitted to crying about them frequently and feeling depressed. She felt she had sacrificed so much for her career and found it hard to understand how people could judge her as undeserving. As a result, it became harder for her to talk to reporters after matches as she dreaded having to replay everything that had occurred in her game, good and bad.

Taking a stand for mental health

In 2021, Naomi ranked second in women's tennis in the world and made the huge decision to refuse to speak with the media at the French Open, citing the toll that news conferences take on athletes' mental health. She shared her views on Instagram and Twitter, "I've often found that people have no regard for athletes' mental health, and this rings true whenever I see a press conference or partake in one." She noted that the repeated questions often bring doubts into the tennis players' minds.

 She reported watching many clips of players crying in the press room after losing matches, a practice she felt lacked any empathy for their well-being and amounted to "kicking a person when they are down." At any rate, she was fined $15,000 for refusing to speak with the Press at the French Open.

Some athletes and public figures like Steph Curry and Serena Williams applauded Naomi's bravery and honesty in prioritizing her own well-being. Mental health professionals also validated her concerns and her decision to initiate a conversation about the mental well-being of athletes and others in high-pressure professional sports. Her transparency helped highlight the need to discuss emotional health without the traditional stigma.

On the other hand, some media figures criticized Naomi for not meeting contractual obligations and for using "mental health as a weapon." Her decision ignited a debate in the media about requiring athletes to discuss their performances.

Becoming a mother

Naomi withdrew from public view during her pregnancy, and in July 2023, she gave birth to a baby girl named Shai with rapper Cordae. She announced a split from Cordae in January 2025, but she has spoken openly about how her pregnancy gave her a break to think about herself and understand her worth outside of tennis, a path toward embracing herself as her own person. Naomi has also shared how being a mother makes her want to make the world a better place for her child. She plans to bring Shai on tour with her when she returns to tennis but is still trying to decide how her career will evolve now that she has a child.

Becoming a mother allowed Naomi to see herself in the big picture and think about the way she could shape her life in new ways. In her video, *The Second Set,* Naomi describes the ways she has approached her career with the big picture in mind, making her mental well-being as a person and a mother a number one priority.

Reflective questions:

How can we protect children and shield ourselves from damaging comments on the internet?

Can Naomi Osaka provide a role model for us all in setting boundaries that protect our well-being?

References:

Coruso, Skyler, "Naomi Osaka Tears Up as She Shares Her Daughter Changed Her Life," posted on People.com, Aug 6, 2025

Sanchez, Rosa, "It Takes More Strength to Speak Up than to Stay Quiet," online article posted June 7, 2022.

Tubi, documentary, produced by Hana Kuma and Nike, *Naomi Osaka: the Second Set,* August 24, 2025.

Best Thing: Inform Yourself about Trauma

"Healing doesn't mean the damage never existed. It means the damage no longer controls our lives."

Ashby Dubay

Darcy couldn't have imagined that her four-year-old son, Ryoma, being involved in a car crash would finally launch her into a new career. It all started when Darcy's best friend, Sherrie, had taken Ryoma to a birthday party while Darcy had to work. After work, she was waiting at home for Sherrie and Ryoma to return home when the police called to say they had been in an accident, and the car they were riding in had been totaled.

The police said they would drive them home after the accident was cleared from the freeway. Four frantic hours later, the police arrived at Darcy's house with Sherrie and Ryoma, and Darcy got to hold her frightened child in her arms. Sherrie said the accident had been harrowing, but fortunately, Ryoma didn't appear to be hurt.

Surviving an Accident

Hearing Sherrie tell the story was overwhelming. Driving home on a crowded Los Angeles freeway, Sherrie had suddenly seen a car pull in front of her. She eased her brakes on slowly to lessen the impact, but then a car traveling 65 miles per hour slammed into her from behind, spinning her car around to face oncoming traffic. Two more cars crashed into Sherrie and Ryoma before the police came. Four-year-old Ryoma screamed hysterically with each crash, begging to get out of his car seat. But Sherrie didn't dare remove him until she was sure the collisions had stopped. In the midst of his terrified crying, the car's airbag exploded, sprinkling white dust over both of them.

Soon, there were sirens, and firemen opened the car door, and once out of danger, they gently asked Ryoma to choose from a big bag of stuffed animals. Ryoma was stunned and couldn't decide between a stuffed tiger and a bear. After picking a bear, he mechanically repeated, "I should have picked the tiger." "I should have picked the tiger."

When Ryoma got home with his bear, Darcy talked with him about the accident and the fact that he was safe now and didn't have to be scared. But Ryoma was still frightened, and when Darcy tried to take Ryoma to the doctor the next morning, he cried and refused to get in the car. Darcy tried countless ways to convince Ryoma that he didn't need to be scared of the car. She talked about their car being safe and walked around it, looking at the gas gauge and checking the tires. Trying to get him into the car took hours, and Darcy was desperate about what to do. She had to take Ryoma to daycare and return to work.

Researching Trauma

As a former actress, Darcy was a good researcher and decided to approach the situation the same way she might have to understand one of her roles. The first remedy she found to quell Ryoma's fears was a technique explained to her by a friend who worked as a professional hypnotist. It was called "tapping therapy" or the Emotional Freedom Technique. EFT was first introduced in the 1990s as an extension of acupuncture, and studies have revealed that it reduces cortisol in the brain.

Learning The Tapping Solution

Darcy's friend taught her how to tap points on Ryoma's head and repeat a calming affirmation out loud, "Even though I'm scared, and I had a bad thing happen in the car, I still like myself." Happily, Ryoma was immediately calmed by the tapping and liked the affirmations.

Within a couple of days, Ryoma felt comfortable getting in the car, and Darcy was convinced they had returned to normal life. However, several months later, she received a call from Ryoma's school stating that he had reacted to the school fire drill in an unusual way. Darcy learned that he had experienced a startle reflex, and he began reacting to all kinds of normal household sounds the same intense way.

Through her research on trauma, Darcy realized that Ryoma's nervous system was still affected by the horrendous sight and sound of the crashes, and although tapping was calming, it wasn't enough to resolve his new symptoms of trauma: the continual startle reactions. Darcy kept researching and discovered that delayed reactions to trauma could be treated by Cognitive Behavioral Therapy. She found a child therapist who helped children reframe reactions to trauma and set up an appointment. At their first session, the therapist asked Ryoma to rate different parts of the accident in terms of how bad he felt when they happened. What were the things that were very bad? Which things felt neutral? Were there some good parts of the event, like the firemen coming? Ryoma drew pictures of his experiences that day and placed each one in the correct column.

Using Hypnosis

Ryoma's startle reactions began to disappear as their therapy sessions went on, and their work released trauma from his body. Gradually, he was able to talk about the accident with more detachment. Consequently, learning about all these treatment modalities changed Darcy as a mother and as a person. She already knew that Ryoma was what's called a highly sensitive person, but now she was learning that there were concrete tools she could use to continue to support his growth. She also grew interested in helping others with trauma. Over the next several years, she studied to become both a hypnotherapist and an early childhood educator. She began to offer private hypnotherapy sessions and to implement trauma-informed care in her classroom. These were meaningful ways she found to serve others.

Reflective questions:

How can parents stay aware of new treatment modalities that can help their children heal from trauma?

Resources:

Phifer, Lisa Weed Ded, NCSP, Sibbald, Laura MA, CCC-SLP, *Trauma-Informed Social- Emotional Toolbox, for Children and Adolescents,* PESI Publishing and Media, May 2020.

Ortner, Nick, *The Tapping Solution: A Revolutionary System for Stress Free Living,* Hay House LLC, September 2014.

Chapter Nine: The Big Picture of Intuitive Decision-making

Saint Francis of Assisi

I met Jeff at a dinner party, where we happened to be seated next to each other. We enjoyed our conversation so much that we decided to share another meal to learn more about each other. Soon, we met for an early dinner at a local restaurant that overlooked a beautiful garden. During two hours of eating and chatting, we confided in each other about events from our childhoods and discovered that we had loved all the same comic books and TV shows. As we talked, we found ourselves enveloped in a warm, ethereal cloud. Both of us wanted to linger over dessert, but I had to rush out to let my babysitter go home. Therefore, saying goodbye in the parking lot was surprisingly poignant, and we agreed we would get together soon.

Reflecting on the evening later, I still felt the warmth of our conversation. However, when I began to ruminate on what we talked about, a red flag popped up. In the course of the evening, Jeff had mentioned that he'd never ever spent time with children and confessed that he hadn't learned to feel comfortable with them. As a singer, he said that he had enjoyed performing for them sometimes, and he had a niece and nephews living in another state, but he seldom got to see them. Those were his only connections with kids. I had never met anyone who had no relationships with children before, and it felt strange. I realized I had a bias and asked myself what it meant: "Who doesn't delight in children?" In my hierarchy of human qualities, loving kids would be near the top. So, I warned myself, "Don't start thinking that Jeff might be "the one."

Nevertheless, Jeff and I felt compelled to keep getting to know each other. We went out for dinners and movies and enjoyed talking for hours on the phone after my kids were in bed. We eventually spoke openly about our love for each other. However, the first time we tiptoed up to the subject of marriage, I felt like a forecaster assessing statistical probabilities. I admitted I was fearful. After recently going through a divorce, I wanted to be certain it wouldn't happen again, and I felt especially protective of my children. I realized that I wanted to be with someone who could grow to love and understand them. How could I even entertain that possibility with Jeff, who had never known any children? In addition, after years of living alone, I couldn't picture him in the clamor of family life.

Somehow, I found it easier to talk to friends about the risk of marriage than to Jeff. Other people were my sounding board, and my friends really liked Jeff, but still cautioned me on decision-making. One of them suggested I lay on my bed and ask myself if marrying Jeff was what I really wanted. She noted that if the answer was yes, I would see a positive symbol, such as colorful balloons. Another friend advised me to list pros and cons. Neither of those ideas produced helpful results. Instead of putting me at ease, it felt way more complicated than that. In fact, in the whirl of my thoughts, the decision sometimes felt impossible.

The process of trying to predict the emotional consequences of a decision is what psychologists refer to as "affective forecasting." When people try to foresee how they will feel in the years to come, it can be challenging because the brain only has access to how they feel in the present moment. It doesn't yet know who the person will become, what emotions they will have in the future. That's why people so often feel stuck grappling with a high-risk decision about the future. The lower mind's nature is to get obsessed with competing possibilities, and that had become my world. Life with Jeff. Life without Jeff. The latter also seemed increasingly impossible.

The Path of Intuition

The way out of the over-thinking mind's machinations is often through intuition, a wavelength of decision-making that we discussed in the first chapter. Intuition involves paying attention to other aspects of perception that allow us access to our inner voice or expand our outlook. Intuition can be triggered by moments of synchronicity or what psychologist Brené Brown calls "God moments." Synchronous events, such as receiving a call from someone we were just thinking about, are common but often don't feel significant in everyday life.

However, when we are dealing with a challenging decision, synchronous events often take on a heightened meaning.

My synchronous moment came in the form of a letter from the wisest person I knew, which included a surprising observation, "I see that Jeff has become your true, dear, and constant friend." Reading his words, I realized I hadn't framed our relationship to honor the deep friendship that existed. My mental chatter obscured that day-to-day reality, but the letter allowed me to see our lives through a wider lens. I realized Jeff was always interested in everything about my life and consistently offered support. My warring predictions slowly dissolved, replaced by feelings of gratitude for Jeff and his wonderful qualities, and I started feeling my way into the intuitive, big-picture understanding of how our lives might evolve.

Forecasters in the financial market talk about trying to envision a cone of possibilities. As Jeff gradually got to know my kids, I noticed that he enjoyed activities with them, and our lives together now seemed full of positive possibilities. We both began to have faith that our future selves would be able to love and support each other, the children, and anyone else who came along.

If you, dear reader, are trying to make a significant decision that will have long-term consequences in your life, have faith that life itself will provide you with moments that allow you to discover your own wisdom and give you a sense of the big picture, as well as glimpses of the person you will become.

Jeff and I couldn't have guessed how many people our decision to marry would ultimately affect – many who weren't even born yet. Over the years, Jeff became the family's favorite person, the one a child wanted to play with, or an adult would go to for sound advice. One of our daughters named their son after him. Our decision to marry rippled through the lives of our children, their partners, our grandchildren, and also through the lives of friends and colleagues. Our decisions ripple into the lives of others because, on the most basic level, we are interconnected.

Decisions That Create Waves in Our Consciousness

I use the image of ripples because sometimes people's choices have a great impact, and their ripples become waves that expand our consciousness and move the world forward. In this chapter, I want to focus on a few of the significant decisions in the lives of three women: Maya Angelou, Pema Chodron, and Brené Brown. They have been change-makers in our cultural and spiritual consciousness, and the way they have lived their lives has helped reframe the ways we see the world.

All three women had children, but their domain of influence hasn't been directly related to their mothering roles, nor did any of them preach about how others should raise their children. In fact, they have sometimes made choices that didn't automatically put their children first. Their decisions emerged from connecting with their own inner voices and facing challenges with authenticity and integrity. However, the new understandings they created will touch children's lives in the future.

I see them as examples of universal mothering. Their life choices help us give birth to new, more compassionate parts of ourselves and develop fresh perspectives on the world. Dear reader, you may have mentors or people you consider mother figures in your life, women who encourage you to be more of who you are. I hope the three women I have chosen as examples of universal mothering will further your abilities to nurture yourself and go beyond the expectations of others to discover your own path.

Maya Angelou and Her Life-Changing Decisions

You may know Maya as the author of *I Know Why the Caged Bird Sings,* The iconic African American poet and author was born Marguerite Johnson in 1928 in St. Louis, Missouri, and spent her formative years in the Jim Crow South. At the age of eight, she was raped by her mother's boyfriend, an event that left her unable to speak for five years. During the period she was mute, Bertha Flowers, a rural librarian, introduced Maya to the wonders of literature and helped her grow her own voice again. Later, Maya became pregnant while still in high school after having sex one time. She was able to hide her pregnancy even from her parents until after her graduation ceremony. Several days after receiving her diploma, she gave birth to a baby whom she named Guy. Although the role of mother didn't become Maya's main identity, she considered Guy a treasure throughout her life.

Maya didn't know how to make her way as a single, black mother. In her book, *"To My Daughter,"* she recounts the story of that transformative period *in* her life. Her mother helped by babysitting Guy sometimes while Maya worked in various jobs, including acting, dancing, and singing, but those jobs didn't offer adequate financial support. When Guy was eight. Maya was invited to join a touring company of *Porgy and Bess* in Europe, but she wasn't able to bring Guy. She reluctantly left her son with her mother while she traveled with the company. She was also able to earn money as a jazz singer in nightclubs and as a dance instructor but sent most of the money home to support her son.

But the benefits of her travel weren't just financial. In Europe, Maya had her first experience of racial tolerance and freedom. She was surprised to discover that she was treated like a talented performer rather than a second-class citizen.

After a few months, Maya started missing Guy fiercely and took on extra jobs to earn passage home. It took several exhausting days of travel to reach her mother's house, but she was thrilled to be united with her son. However, after a week back in America, Maya experienced debilitating culture shock. She felt overwhelmed by the racist attitudes she had been used to in the past. Europe had offered her the vision of what it might mean to raise a child with freedom and self-worth. Suddenly, Maya was seized by the idea that it would be better to kill herself and her son so they could escape the suffocation of that oppression.

The Decision to Stay Alive and Raise Her Son

She ran out of the house and took a taxi to a local mental health facility, where she told the woman at the receptionist desk that it was an emergency. She needed to see a therapist immediately. She was directed to an office staffed by a young white man. His obvious lack of understanding of her situation resulted in even more hopelessness, and she cried without uttering a word. Maya then left the clinic and took a taxi to her voice teacher's house. When he answered the door, she expressed all the desperation about her life and said she wanted to commit suicide. Her voice teacher, a well-known charismatic figure whom she greatly respected, stayed calm. He told her he was with another voice student and directed her to another room, where he gave her firm instructions.

He put a yellow legal tablet and pen on the table. He instructed her to write down all the things she had to be grateful for in her life: the ability to hear music, to see flowers, to love other people, and not to stop writing until she had noted everything. Maya wrote and wrote, filling the whole pad, and on the last page, she added, "I am blessed." The process changed Maya's thinking and launched her into a new chapter of her life. She could see the big picture and realized how fortunate she was, so she decided, on the spot, to practice gratitude every day.

In the future, Maya would go on to write countless poems, articles, and books that would expand people's thinking in unprecedented ways, but she began every piece of writing on a yellow pad with the words, "I am blessed." Although she never earned a degree beyond high school, she went on to receive fifty honorary degrees from colleges all across the country. However, she didn't begin her pivotal writing project until decades after her reorientation by her voice teacher, and by then, she had become a revered figure in the Civil Rights Movement.

The Decision to Share the Shameful Secrets of Her Life

In the 1960s, Maya was living with Guy in Harlem, where she was part of the literary scene and recognized as an important activist. At that time, Harlem was a hub of artistic and civil rights activity, and she was friends with both the renowned writer James Baldwin and Civil Rights leader Dr. Martin Luther King. However, tragedy struck on Maya's birthday, April 4, 1968, when King was assassinated in Memphis, Tennessee. Like the rest of America, Maya was shocked, and she became seriously depressed. Baldwin and an editor friend urged Angelou to move through her depression by writing about her life in the style of a fiction book. This felt daunting to her, but they persisted. Both men thought that taking on the project would help heal her grief and remind her of her own resilience.

Maya finally made the momentous decision to share the story of her early life. She entitled the book *I Know Why the Caged Bird Sings,* and she worked on it so quickly that it was published nine months after King's assassination, on January 1, 1969. Her book revealed all the chapters of her young life: the year she and her older brother Bailey were cared for by her grandmother in Stamps, Arkansas, the tragedy of rape, the years of silence, and the miraculous teacher who lured her into literature and taught her to cultivate her literary voice.

Ultimately, I *Know Why the Caged Bird Sings* sold over two million copies and had a huge impact on national consciousness. As the first popular autobiography of an African American woman, it raised awareness of the oppression of growing up with systemic racism and sexism. Still, it also revealed the power of optimism and resilience. Over the years, the book has become a staple in high school English classes, although in recent times, there have been attempts to ban it.

Oprah Winfrey read the book the year it was published, when she was fifteen, and remembers it changed her life. "The whole world fell away from me. That book gave a voice to my silences and my secrets." It was the first book Oprah had ever read that had a black protagonist, and she found that Maya's narrative mirrored her own. Oprah, too, had been raised in poverty, struggled as the daughter of a single mom in a culture that considered her inferior, but went on to develop a strong sense of self and purpose. Today, we recognize the vital role of diverse characters in children's books, ensuring that every child feels seen and understood, and learns to appreciate and understand others. We also recognize the power of role models who enable us to face adversity more resiliently. Maya's book changed our nation's consciousness.

The wave of inspirational thought Maya created was expressed beautifully in the original poem she wrote in 1978 and recited at Bill Clinton's inauguration. In her deep, resonant voice, Maya repeated the poem's title *And Still I Rise,* with every stanza. Her voice carried the message for all who have endured life's setbacks and found the strength to gone on.

Her ability to offer universal mothering to everyone was expressed in her book A *Letter to My Daughter* published in 2009. The book begins with Maya's explanation that, although she never gave birth to a girl, she considered every woman, regardless of race or income bracket, to be her daughter. On the last page, Maya thanks women by name who mothered her in this life and expresses her appreciation to those who had considered her their spiritual mother. Her expressions of deep connections and gratitude to others are a shining example of women's abilities to mentor and nurture one another.

In the wave of consciousness that Maya created, we gain a fuller glimpse of the need for an endlessly elastic compassion for others and for ourselves. The next woman we will explore also brought compassion to the forefront of our society's consciousness. You may know Pema Chodren as an author and Buddhist teacher. She was born only a few years after Maya Angelou, but she was raised in a very different cultural environment.

Pema Chodron And Her Life-Changing Decisions

Pema was born Deirdre Bloomfield and grew up on a farm in New Jersey with wealthy parents. As a child of privilege, she was sent to the prestigious Miss Porter's School for girls in Farmington, Connecticut, which had a reputation for encouraging academic rigor and strong character. She continued on to Sarah Lawrence College, an elite institution, where she earned her bachelor's degree. At twenty-one, Deirdre met and married a young lawyer, and they had two children, a daughter, Arlyn, and a son, Edward. The couple moved to California, where Deirdre earned a degree in elementary education at the University of California, Berkeley, and started teaching.

However, the couple eventually separated, and Deirdre went through the pain of a divorce. Nevertheless, she married again, this time to a writer, and moved with her new husband, and children, Arlyn, and Edward to Mexico for a couple of years, then to Taos, New Mexico, where she resumed teaching. In the 1960s, Taos had become a hub of artistic and counter-culture activities, which existed alongside the vibrant, traditional life of the Taos Pueblo. Deirdre enjoyed life in Taos and occasionally attended sweat lodges as part of the rich, cross-fertilized cultural life there. Everything in her world was peaceful and relaxed until one day, a shocking event shattered her sense of identity and any remaining stability.

It happened when she was sitting outside peacefully drinking tea. Her husband came around the corner of the house, and during what she expected to be a casual conversation, he confessed that he had been having an affair, actually several affairs, and planned to leave her. In a video describing the event, she later said, "This so undid me.

Something happens that annihilates you, and I felt so much terror at my anger." She talks about her habitual sense of herself as easygoing and mild-mannered and how that amiable self was wiped out by her husband's confession, as if by a storm that leaves nothing in its wake. She floundered about trying to find a way out of her feeling of groundlessness and dabbled in different therapies. But she was flooded with fantasies of burning down the woman's house, who was involved with her husband, and of hurting him. It was an inner violence that she had never experienced, and she had no idea how to move through it and regain a stable perspective on life.

The Decision to Understand Negativity

Then one day, Deirdre experienced a synchronous moment when someone gave her an article entitled "Working with Negativity" by a Tibetan Buddhist master. The article explained that there was nothing wrong with difficult emotions and that, in fact, they could be a force to awaken a person spiritually. The problems with negativity, it stated, were the human tendencies to blame others or oneself. The article was Deirdre's introduction to Buddhism and the concepts of non-duality, where things are not judged as good or bad.

Reading it again and again helped Deirdre to believe the negative force she was feeling held the key to another whole sphere of life. Her passion to understand these ideas more deeply prompted her to fly to the French Alps and then to London for short periods of Buddhist study. As a result, she made an unprecedented decision. Despite being an American woman and mother, she chose to become a Tibetan Buddhist nun. A year later, with two teenagers still living at home, she was formally initiated. Although others might have criticized her, Deirdre followed her intuition, and her teacher gave her the name Pema Chodron, which translates as "the lotus torch of the dharma" or "the lamp of truth."

In a 2009 interview with Oprah Winfrey, Pema discussed how the decision affected her children at the time. She said that Arlyn had experienced some feelings of rejection, though Edward claimed he hadn't been affected by it. Over the years, Pema worked to repair her relationship with Arlyn. This is a good role model for mothers who want to make amends after they go through a stressful period of life that affects their children. In retrospect, it had been a tumultuous time for the whole family, but she still felt that her intuition to become a Buddhist nun was so powerful that she couldn't have chosen otherwise.

As a result of her Buddhist training, she found a profound inner stability and felt inspired to share her discoveries of mindfulness with anyone who would listen. In 1991, she authored the book *The Wisdom of No Escape.* In 1996, she revisited some of the themes that had led her to Buddhism during the tumultuous times in a book called *When Things Fall Apart: Heart Advice for Difficult Times.* It became a bestseller and is widely acclaimed as the most popular book ever written about navigating life's challenges. In all, Pema has written several books that have been read by millions of people and is seen as uniquely qualified to help a broad audience understand and manage difficult emotions.

Undoubtedly, the wave of consciousness that Pema Chodron created through her writing and workshops continues to help people handle adversity with resilience and compassion. It has also made the principles of mindfulness popular in parenting and everyday life. When you try to practice mindfulness and resilience, you are, in an essential way, channeling the pioneering work of Pema Chodron. Like Maya Angelou, she is recognized by a great many as one of the universal mothers of our time, someone who can help people respond to challenges in self-reflective, intuitive ways.

That brings us to our third woman, who has also been a force in helping us view ourselves and others with more understanding and compassion. You may know Brené Brown as the author of the best-selling book, *Atlas of the Heart.* Brene comes from yet another cultural sphere - the Deep South. Her research and public presentations have introduced us to the roles that shame, vulnerability, and empathy play in our internal lives and in our connections to others.

Brené Brown and Her Life-Changing Decisions

Brené grew up in the 1960s and 1970s in the deep South culture of Texas and Louisiana. The oldest of four children, she earned her BA at the University of Texas at Austin. Brené enjoyed delving into exciting new psychological research in her undergraduate program as well as the lively party life at the school. In 1996, she was about to graduate and go on to graduate school, and it felt like clear sailing, but Brené didn't know that she was on the brink of a life-changing decision. One of the required projects for graduation was to construct a psychological/social genogram, a pictorial review of her family history, the kind of exploration of heritage described in the second chapter of this book.

Brené approached the assignment with enthusiasm and a sense of curiosity. She called her mother and asked her to talk about the lives of her grandparents and great-grandparents. They spent a long time on the phone delving deep into their family history. Brené, however, found the details about her ancestors' lives disturbing, and at the end of the conversation, she said, "Jesus, Mom, what the hell?" Her mother agreed that she knew the stories were upsetting because she had been part of them. But as a budding psychological researcher, Brené realized that many of the stories that had been previously described to her as "hard living" actually indicated addiction and mental health problems. It was still true that there were wonderful tales of resilience and triumph, but there were an equal number that revealed severe trauma and alcoholism. Creating the genogram unraveled everything Brown knew about her family history, and in addition, the process motivated her to shine a light on her own propensities for addiction, something she had never considered.

The Decision to Adopt Sobriety

Over the course of two weeks, Brené reflected intensively on her life to date. Did she drink too much? What about eating to numb difficult feelings? What about smoking to calm her nerves when she was under stress, which turned out to be daily. She finally arrived at a life choice that would have shocked her weeks earlier: to stop drinking and smoking overnight and join Alcoholics Anonymous. It wasn't the way she expected her post-master's life to unfold, but she totally embraced her newfound freedom from chemical dependence by dedicating herself to attending AA meetings.

However, she wasn't sure if she was an alcoholic, so in the first weeks of AA, she got a sponsor who diagnosed her with a web of addictions, including drinking, smoking, and emotional eating. The sponsor advised Brené to quit all of them. In addition, she told her to stop trying to manage and control family crises. Brené discussed her

23 years of sobriety in an online article. She remembers that when she decided to stop drinking, she feared all the magic would go out of life but actually discovered just the opposite. Enjoying the little things in everyday life clearly and authentically became the new magic, and she credits her sobriety with making her success possible. She is also proud that her decision to adopt sobriety as a college graduate prepared her to raise her children to regard alcohol consumption in a cautious, thoughtful way. Her article celebrating her sobriety describes the effective ways she taught boundaries regarding alcohol to her children.

After earning her PhD at the University of Houston, Brené's research into the provocative subjects of shame, vulnerability, empathy, and courage gained widespread recognition within academic and social circles. In fact, her work had received so much attention that when TEDx was about to start up in Houston in 2010, they invited her to be their first speaker on any subject she chose. Brené decided to discuss her favorite research subject: vulnerability. Her talk, *The Power of Vulnerability,* became an instant web-video phenomenon, watched and shared by millions of people. That's when Brené's success exploded and became, however, unexpectedly complicated. She was delighted at the huge response but unprepared for what followed.

When she and her husband, Steve, saw how many people had watched the talk and continued to do so, he suggested that she bask in those feelings of accomplishment and refrain from looking at online comments. He didn't mention why. One day, when Steve and their children were away, Brené couldn't resist looking online, and she started reading. She recalls a few comments that contained constructive feedback, such as suggesting that addressing the subject of vulnerability should include a discussion of the role of trust, an idea she found helpful.

The Decision to Stay in the Arena

However, Brené was overwhelmed and as she read further, she was shocked by the mean-spirited comments that targeted her personally, making her want to withdraw from public appearances. People had posted comments about her, such as, "She definitely needs Botox." "She should lose fifteen pounds." "How can her husband and children stand the way she looks?" "She should die." Although Brené thought that theoretically she should be able to ignore hate speech, she had a visceral reaction that day that cast her into a vortex of shame and confusion.

She described how she attempted to find a way to cope in the hours after reading those statements in her 2019 Netflix special titled *"The Call to Courage."* She admits to taking a jar of peanut butter and a spoon and watching Downton Abbey reruns for hours. When she ran out of episodes, Brené started googling facts about what was happening in the world during the program's historical period. One of the random questions she asked online was, "Who was president of the United States during the Downton Abbey era?" The answer popped up: Theodore Roosevelt. An avid researcher, she immediately began searching for information about Roosevelt. Then something amazingly synchronistic occurred. She discovered a talk Roosevelt gave back in 1910 at the Sorbonne and was electrified when she read that in his speech, he had used the term "daring greatly" to describe those who choose to stay in the arena of life, rather than join others who sit on the sidelines and criticize.

When all her impulses cried out for her to withdraw from the world, those words were like a life raft, and she describes coming upon the phrase "daring greatly" as her moment of epiphany. It gave her a glimpse of what vulnerability might mean in her career going forward in the big picture. Brené asked herself a life-changing question: how can one contribute actively to society while remaining human and vulnerable, with the risk of getting one's feelings hurt?

Roosevelt provided a role model for staying in the arena and giving attention to those offering positive contributions. Part of her decision involved putting more emphasis on her work on vulnerability rather than shame, which was complicated for people to understand. To honor her inspiration, she titled her next book, which was published in 2012, *"Daring Greatly: How the Courage to Be Vulnerable Transforms the Way We Live, Love, Parent, and Lead."*

That was just the start. In 2018, she published *"Darring to Lead."* In 2020 came *Atlas of the Heart,* and in 2021, *You Are Your Best Thing: Vulnerability, Shame, and Resilience in the Black Experience* with Tarana Burke. Currently, she is a professor at the University of Houston, where she holds the Huffington Foundation Endowed Chair and serves as a visiting professor at the University of Texas at Austin's School of Business.

Through her courageous work and decisions, she has helped society redefine vulnerability as a strength and a key to genuine connection with others. The subject of shame is also vitally important to mothers who so frequently experience negative self-talk when they are criticized by others or compare themselves in unrealistic ways. Understanding shame in an everyday sense is crucial for helping children maintain their self-worth when they receive negative feedback. As mothers, we also want to be role models of vulnerability when we repair conflicts with our children. The ripples that come from Brené's work lie at the core of our lives. She has been a powerful role model, enabling all to embrace their own imperfections and prioritize mental health in their families and work environments.

Today, we can't effectively separate our own values and ideas from the role models of these three very public women and the change they brought about through their private struggles. Their courage to reveal their lives for all to see helps provide inspiration and practical tools for our own transformations. However, it's not just about them; it's about you and countless other women making decisions that ripple into our lives.

Dear reader, please know that your decision-making process is equally precious and, in some sense, bigger than you are. Decisions that involve challenges will inevitably arise in your life and propel you on your journey. I invite you to reflect on and write about some significant decisions you have made and how they have affected your awareness.

Now, where are a few concluding stories of the book, examples of courageous and intuitive decision-making. Each of the three stories highlights the reality that the myth of the perfect parent doesn't prepare us for the eventualities that occur in our lives. Although difficult things happened to each of the following women, in a real sense, the challenges they faced allowed them to come into the fullness of their own being and make meaningful contributions to the world._ The decisions of the women in these stories occurred in different life circumstances and time periods.

The first story starts in the 1960s in San Francisco, where Joan Brann's dedication to improving her community is interrupted by a tragedy in the life of her teenage son and the subsequent death of her husband. Despite her mental duress, she decides to move across the country, where she knows she has no family or friends, but experiences a life-changing synchronous event.

The second story takes place in the 1970s, when Betty Ford, a former dancer, became a reluctant first lady who just wanted her private life back. However, during two lifequakes, she decides to share her most personal problems with the public and, as a result, changes national consciousness.

In the third story, Ann Lamott teaches us about love, not just for our children no matter how they are faring, but most importantly for ourselves, when we are overstretched to meet their needs, even as adults. She shows what happens when we make the radical choice to fall in love with ourselves.

Reflective questions:

Have there been life choices that seemed impossible to you at a particular time?

What decisions have you made that took you on a new path of learning?

Are there people whose decisions you admire?

Resources:

Angelou, Maya, *And Still I Rise,* Caged Bird Legacy, 1978.

Angelou, Mayra, *I Know Why the Caged Bird Sings,* Reissue edition, Ballantine, 2009.

Brown, Brené, *Atlas of the Heart,* Random House, 2021.

Brown, Brené, *Dare to Lead, Brave Work, Tough Conversations, Whole Hearts*, Random House, 2018.

Brown, Brené, *Daring Greatly: How the Courage to be Vulnerable Transforms the Way We Live,* Avery, 2015.

Brown, Brené, "What Being Sober has Meant to Me," online article, May 31, 2019.

Brown, Brené, *The Call to Courage,* Netflix, 2019.

Brown, Brené, *The Power of Vulnerability,* TED Talk, June 2010,

Celestine, Nicole, PhD, Scientifically reviewed by Smith, William, "What is Affective Forecasting? A Psychologist Explains," Positive Psychology, September 2018.

Cherry, Kendra, M.S.Ed, *The Everything Psychology Book: An Introductory Guide to the Science of Human Behavior, Everything, 2010.*

Chödrön, Pema, "Why I Became a Buddhist" YouTube, Sounds True, Feb 14, 2008.

Chödrön, Pema, *When Things Fall Apart*: *Heart Advice for Difficult Times,* Shambhala, 2000.

Chödrön, Pema, *The Wisdom of No Escape,* Shambala, 2011.

Gladwell, Malcolm, *Blink, The Power of Thinking Without Thinking,* Back Bay Books, April 2007.

Maidenberg, Michelle, PhD, MPH, LCSW, R. CGP, "6 Tips for Making Difficult Decisions. Challenging Decisions Often Pit our Core Values against Each Other," Psychology Today, online article, March 10, 2021.

Oprah, "Oprah Talks to Pema Chodron," Interview, *2019.*

Kahneman, Daniel, *Thinking Fast and Slow,* Farrar, Straus and Giroux, April 2013.

Plessner, Henning, Betsch, Cornelia, Betsch, Tillman, Editors, *Intuition in Judgment and Decision Making,* Psychology Press, October 2007.

Trungpa, Chögyam. *The Myth of Freedom and the Way of Meditation.* Shambhala Books, 1976.

Best Things: Work for Community Health

"Be the change you want to see."

Mahatma Gandhi

Even though Joan Brann was a single mother, she was a major player in bringing about change in San Francisco's African American community in the 1960's. But major life events left her wondering if she could go on. Her children were proud of her community organizing abilities from a young age. At the age of twelve, her son Michael asked her when she was going to run for governor. His little sister, Shaun, was also amazed by what her mother did, and both children accompanied her when she volunteered at various political events. Born in Oakland, California, Joan, however, had no aspirations to be a politician; she was, however, committed to positive social action and found herself at the center of organizing for civil rights issues in San Francisco's political scene.

Building A Better Community

In 1963, she became the first African American of either gender to hold a position in the California Democratic Party, when she was elected organizational secretary. Her progress in organizing politically began when she decided to take action about the poor garbage service in her Western Addition, San Francisco, neighborhood. She brought her complaints to the Democratic Council and got results. She continued to fight tirelessly for several issues, including fair housing, equal employment, and any cause for the disenfranchised. After attending a conference in Fresno, she became a staunch supporter of migrant farm workers and stopped eating grapes for several years due to the way workers were treated. She also joined the Black Women Organized for Political Action (BWOPA) and sponsored an event for Coretta King when she came to San Francisco.

Joan assisted in Willie Brown's political campaigns as he prepared to run for mayor of San Francisco, an elected position he held from 1996 to 2004. As a single, divorced parent and full-time legal secretary, Joan explained her devotion to volunteering, "It's the best way I know to make the world a better place for my children." She was indeed devoted to her children and did everything to make their home a happy one. She even learned to sew in order to create clothes and beautiful bedspreads for her children.

Then, her family grew. In 1964, Joan married a lawyer named Franklyn Brann and became a stepmother to three other children, ranging in age from 3 to 15. Her nineteen-year-old son, Michael, became a father to a baby girl named Rahmana, and Joan was thrilled that he was continuing in his studies at UC Berkeley, where he was a good student and very socially conscious. He had become part of an organization that was affiliated with the Black Panthers. The Black Panther Party was founded in Oakland in 1966. They implemented many positive community programs, including complimentary breakfasts for children, clothing distribution, and transportation services. They also patrolled neighborhoods, monitoring excessive police force against African Americans.

Coping with an Unexpected Tragedy

One day, Michael was involved in a disturbance with a policeman and, fearing that he would be blamed, immediately fled to Cuba. Joan was shocked especially when she realized she had no way to visit her firstborn child because of the hostile relationship at the time between the US and Cuba. In 1963, the US had started restricting any legal travel to Cuba. She was filled with feelings of loss. The same year, Joan's father was diagnosed with cancer. It was a terrible year, but she found joy when her daughter, Shaun, gave birth to a little girl named Rudishoa. She decided to focus on her own growth, and she returned to San Francisco State University to complete her BA in Sociology and subsequently matriculated with an MBA at Lone Mountain College.

With the help of a close friend who owned a newspaper called the Sun Reporter, Joan was able to visit Michael in Cuba in 1976. Joan bravely traveled to Cuba through Mexico and was at last reunited with her son. However, her joy was short-lived. While she was visiting Michael, Franklyn suddenly passed away, leaving her a widow at the age of forty-five, and Joan left for home immediately to plan her husband's memorial. When Joan arrived back home, although surrounded by family and loving friends, she still felt overwhelmed by her grief. As a result, she had to decide whether to withdraw from life and just rest or try to continue with her active life.

Creating a New Life

Joan was always a fighter. She decided to think in terms of the big picture and continue working to improve her community, her city, and even her country. This is highlighted by the fact that in 1977, Jimmy Carter asked Joan to take on the position of director of the San Francisco International Reception Center. She accepted the invitation and, with dignity and joy, hosted visitors from all over the world. In due time, she was offered the prestigious role of Director of the African American Institute in Washington, DC, and bravely decided to move there. She would always view that decision as one of her synchronous blessings.

While she was living in the nation's capital, someone lent her a book that changed her life. It was a large, hardcover book featuring a portrait of a beguiling Indian man on the cover, titled *How a Master Works*. The book was written by Ivy O. Duce, the Murshida, or spiritual director, of Sufism Reoriented, an organization founded by the Indian spiritual master Meher Baba. Joan had never heard of Meher Baba or Ivy Duce, but the book enthralled her. It detailed Ivy Duce's life and spiritual journey, focusing on her personal meeting with Meher Baba and her devotion and work for him as the leader of Sufism. The book was filled with fascinating anecdotes and stories about saints and masters from various spiritual and religious traditions. Receiving the book was a synchronous moment for Joan, who had been a seeker all her life, and she became a follower of Meher Baba and a member of Sufism Reoriented.

Fighting Drug Use

In 1982, after two years in Washington, Joan returned to California and was delighted to take up residence in Oakland, the city where she was born. After moving into a nice home in what she thought was a good residential neighborhood, she discovered that her hometown had undergone significant changes over the years. Crack cocaine had become widely available in Oakland, leading to a surge in drug use and an epidemic of addiction. Joan was outraged to see drug dealers actively pursuing deals right in her quiet neighborhood and felt she had to do something about it. The drug trade was affecting children, with some using marijuana or crack cocaine at a young age.

Her community organizing skills kicked into gear, and she founded a new organization called *Oakland Parents in Action*. She traveled to Oakland schools and spoke with the children and their parents. At one school, Joan asked, "What would you do if someone offered you drugs?" A child answered, "Just say no!' and a vibrant slogan was born. Later, First Lady Nancy Reagan took on the cause of drug abuse. Joan invited her to attend an Oakland Parents in Action event, and Nancy loved the phrase "Just Say No," adopting it as the slogan for her national anti-drug work.

Settling in with Family

In her personal life, Joan was able to visit Michael in Cuba several times and to meet her granddaughters, Yhonnia and Antara. One of them appeared in an acrobatics class featured in the documentary "The Buena Vista Social Club." Years later, Joan moved to Vallejo to be near her daughter, Shaun, and they opened a business together, enjoying their happy collaboration for several years. Before she died in 2018, she had gotten to know two great-grandchildren, Lali and Noah.

The decisions Joan made, even during events that might incapacitate someone less resilient, were all based on love and a desire to serve others. As a result, her memorial was flooded with people who had experienced her nurturing, generous presence at different times in their lives, and they wanted to offer their thanks for the privilege of knowing her.

In the long run, Joan's legacy had nothing to do with politics. She began by trying to change her community through the Democratic Party, and later in life, her biggest community project was achieved alongside a Republican First Lady. Joan created ripples that inspired people to believe in public service wherever she went.

Reflective questions:

What gives women the resilience to go on after devastating losses?

Resources:

Duce, Ivy, *How A Master Works,* Sufism Reoriented, 1975.

Richardson, Shaun, *Joan Brann's life,* PDF.

Best thing: Stay True to Your Values

"That's what we're here for here on this Earth, to help others." Betty Ford

Betty Ford was not happy when her husband, Gerald, went from House minority leader to vice president, and she certainly never wanted him to be president. However, on August 8, 1974, Richard Nixon announced that he would be the first US president to resign, and on August 9, Gerald Ford was sworn in as the 38th President of the United States. Things happened so fast that they couldn't even move into the White House right away.

The Decision to Reveal a Shameful Diagnosis

One month later, in September, Betty went for a routine gynecological examination, and the doctors told her that they had found a lump in her breast. Although breast cancer wasn't discussed publicly, everyone knew in 1974 that a diagnosis was usually a death sentence. Betty, her three children, and the president were all terrified. According to the medical procedures of the day, Betty was told that while she was under anesthesia, they would do a biopsy, and if the lump was malignant, they would perform a mastectomy while she was still asleep.

Counter to the practices of the day, Betty insisted that the White House issue a public statement about the procedure. The doctors performed a radical mastectomy, removing the breast and lymph nodes. Photographers publicized pictures of Betty afterward, one cheerfully tossing a football to her husband. The articles about her treatment and surgery provided the general public with some of its first comprehensive information about breast cancer, and the first lady received 35,000 letters from the public supporting her. Moreover, thousands of women across the country underwent mammograms. As the mother of three children, with an avalanche of responsibilities, Betty needed help.

Clara Powell was an allomother for Betty and her children, and she devotes a whole chapter in her book to Clara's mothering of her children, called, *The Other Woman.* She writes, "…in a way, she was their mother. In a way, she was also my mother." Betty was an active second lady and an outspoken one on many issues, like abortion and tolerance of others, and she could stay true to her values and do it all because she knew Clara was loving and supporting her children.

Betty worked tirelessly on the campaign for the Equal Rights Amendment and was devastated when it failed to pass. She was given pain medication for a debilitating condition from arthritis and a pinched nerve earlier in her husband's career. She was also open with the reporters that she took pain pills and valium three times a day to help her relax. In those days, valium was widely prescribed to women and was called "mothers' little helper." Between 1969 and 1982, valium was the most prescribed drug in the United States, and sales in 1978 soared to $2.3 billion. Like most people in Washington, Betty enjoyed cocktails at the end of the day. These were ways that Betty eased her wildly busy life as First Lady for the 895 days her husband was President. Leaving public life turned out to be surprisingly difficult.

The Decision to Reveal Addiction

After Ford lost to Jimmy Carter in 1976, he and Betty moved to a comfortable home in Rancho Mirage, California. Ford continued a busy travel schedule, helping his party even after leaving office, leaving Betty at home all day to adjust to a whole new lifestyle with almost nothing to do. On April 1, 1978, Ford's youngest child, Susan, her two brothers, Betty's assistant, the ex-president, and a physician staged an intervention with Betty, confronting her about her addiction to pain pills and her use of alcohol. Betty was shocked and furious but agreed to go into a rehab facility.

For most people this would be a well-guarded secret. What did Betty decide to do? In an era when no one discussed these issues publicly, she announced that she had a problem with addiction and was going into a rehab facility. At that time, there weren't many rehab facilities for people to enter, and Betty had to go into one run by the Navy. In the beginning, she didn't agree that she had a problem with alcohol, only the pills, but after spending two weeks in rehab, she realized that she had an issue with alcoholism and announced it to the public. Betty's openness helped the public learn that women also suffered from addiction, and that it didn't have to involve shame.

A year after her own intervention, she participated in one with her neighbor, Leonard Firestone, former president of Firestone Rubber. He had the idea that they could open a rehabilitation center together, but she was hesitant at first, fearing it would be embarrassing if she relapsed. However, she went ahead and founded the Betty Ford Rehab Center in 1982. Betty played an active role in supporting patients in nurturing ways until her death in 2011. Her openness about difficult issues still ripples through our lives today.

Reflective questions:

How did Betty maintain her own personal values even though her husband was involved in public life?

How does the bravery of women to share private events in their lives help others?

References:

Ford Betty with Chase, Chris, *The Times of My Life*, Harper and Row, 1978.

Best Thing: Fall in Love with Yourself

"Your children are not your children. They are the sons and daughters of Life's longing for itself. They come through you but not from you, and though they are with you, yet they belong not to you."

Khalil Gibran

How do we preserve our well-being even when our children are going through a period when they are not doing well? When Ann LaMott's beloved son, Sam, was about eighteen, he got involved with things that deeply concerned her: drinking, smoking pot, and using methamphetamines. Ann felt it wasn't working living in the same house, so she rented him an apartment nearby. After a little while, Sam invited a young woman named Amy to move in with him, and a year and a half later, Ann learned Amy was going to have a baby. At that point, Sam had a steady job in San Francisco, and to help them provide a stable home for their new baby, she rented a place for them there.

 Ann saw the baby often and sometimes even took care of him overnight. She also provided emotional triage. When Sam and Amy argued, each turned to her separately for support. Ann listened to Amy and Sam in loving, encouraging ways. When they finally split up, Ann was worried about their little boy, so she invited Amy and the baby to move in with her. However, Ann was still concerned about Sam after the separation and called Bonnie, the spiritual mentor she had consulted for years, to get her perspective on the situation. Bonnie said bluntly, "You need to put Sam in God's hands and retire from the role of being a higher power in his life." But Sam's use of drugs escalated. After this conversation, she made a devastating decision. She told Sam he couldn't enter her house to see his baby unless he was clean and sober. It was an extremely hard decision, and in addition, Sam was angry. Then one day, he called and announced he had been sober for ten days and was getting help from other men who were working on the same issues. He asked if he could come over and visit the baby, and she gave a triumphant, "Yes!" Ann still remembers that glorious, amazing day. Her decision had helped both of them.

Stretching to be there for everyone

However, even after Amy moved out of Ann's house, Ann, as the mother-figure for both of them, still played the exhausting role of supporting them both emotionally. One day, the whole process pushed Ann over the edge. Both Sam and Amy had criticized her about their own issues in two different phone calls, and Ann started crying uncontrollably. She was so upset that she had to get out of the house, so she got in the car and drove around shouting how much she hated everyone. Eventually, she drove back home, pulled into a side street, and called Bonnie.

Bonnie was happy Anne had finally come to understand that she had needs that she was neglecting in order to take care of her adult child and his family. She told Ann she had reached a similar point with her own grown children, realizing she needed to make herself a priority. No one else could do it for her. Essentially, Bonnie told Ann she had to stop taking care of everyone else and start showering herself with love, as if she were her own romantic partner. Ann responded that she wouldn't know where to start. Buy herself a corsage? Cook herself a great dinner?

Deciding to become her own love interest

However, she decided to try it and practiced loving and nurturing herself every day for months. That's when Neal, the man she married, showed up. She tells that.and much more in her book, *Somehow: Thoughts on Love,* which is a treasure trove of ruminations about how life doesn't always make sense, but love is the remedy. Love for ourselves. Messy love with others. And for Ann, love of Jesus or a higher power is central, and she often writes about her spiritual insights.

As Ann reveals in her book, in the big picture, our significant decisions always involve love on some level. Life's challenges pose a question again and again, "Can we love ourselves and be reliant on our inner voice to make choices that align with our highest knowing, even when we make mistakes and fail? How do we create our own well-being instead of depending on others to do it for us? Ann LaMott is a wonderful storyteller, and her humor, honesty, and wisdom ripples through us and supports us in recognizing our own humanness and, in so doing, cherish each step of our learning.

Dear reader, I celebrate the fact that your story is still in process. I hope you will love yourself through all your challenges and believe in your own abilities to protect and cherish your well-being and, if you are a mother, the very unique being that is your child.

Reflective questions:

How can we love our children and set boundaries at the same time?

Do you have someone like Bonnie in your life who helps you remember to pay attention to your own needs and love yourself?

Can you see that in the big picture, you and your child are both on a journey of learning?

Resource:

LaMott, Ann, *Somehow,* Riverhead Books, 2024.

Acknowledgements:

Showers of gratitude:

To Jeff, for tirelessly reading page after page with love, encouragement, and a remarkable understanding of words;

To my baby sister, Andrea, an endless source of talent and creativity, for your vision of the "big picture" and your dedication to turning it into the most whimsical cover;

To dearest Ellen Baum, for believing so strongly in the value of bringing compassion to mothers;

To the patient, elegant Allen Shulakoff, the endlessly encouraging Sarah Collins, and Anna Hoffman, and Logan Walsh, for always seeing the big picture of the book;

To the bright lights in my life: Matty, Lana, Gabby, Peter, Mari, Phokham, Malakai, Lila, Mila, Ollie, and Anjali, for teaching and inspiring me every day.

My biggest thanks to every one of my beloved storytellers and inspirers. Each of your narratives and brilliant ideas will live in my heart forever.

Abby, Allen, Amy B, Amy O, Alicia Jo, Andrea N, Andrea S, Ann, Anna, Annette, Annie D, Arwen, Aunt Betty, Bianca, Bob, Brad, Brene, Catherine N, Catherine P, Caryl, Chrisy, Christy, Corinna, Cynthia, Darcy, Debbie, Depika, Donald, Elif, Elizabeth, Emily, Ethan, Francis, Frida, Gabby, Giulia, Glennon, Gulnar, Gwen, Hannah B, Haylene, Harriet, Howie, Ivy, Jennifer, Jodie, Judith, Kathleen, Katie O, Katie R, Katrinca, Kevin, Kim W, Kristin, Janet, Jayne, Jen, Jennifer, Joan B, Joan R, Jodie, Joseph, Katie O, Lana, Lauren, Linda, Lucia, Magda, Marshall, Mari, Mark, Marshall, Marti, Mary C, Mary Louise. Mary N, Mary C, Maya, Megan M,, Mimi, Mister Rogers, Naomi, Nari,, Nora, Pema, Prescott, Quincy, Rachel, Rani, Robyn, Ronald, Rosangela, Sarah K, Sarah H, Serena, Shauna R, Shauna T, Shelley K, Stephanie, Suriya, Tren, Vicki A, Wendy D, and Wendy W.

9 7989 0190 1090